Moses Cordovero's Introduction to Kabbalah: An Annotated Translation of His *Or Ne'erav*

by

Ira Robinson

The Michael Scharf Publication Trust
of the Yeshiva University Press
New York

KTAV Publishing House, Inc
Hoboken, NJ

Sources and Studies in
Kabbalah, Hasidism, and Jewish Thought, Vol. III.

Volume I: Torah Lishmah: Torah for Torah's Sake in the Works of Rabbi Hayyim of Volozhin and his Contemporaries by *Norman Lamm*

Volume II: All Is in the Hands of Heaven: The Teachings of Rabbi Mordecai Joseph Lerner of Izbica by *Morris M. Faierstein*

Volume III: Moses Cordovero's Introduction to Kabbalah: An Annotated Translation of His *Or Ne'erav* by *Ira Robinson*

Edited by Norman Lamm
President and Jakob and Erna Michael
Professor of Jewish Philosophy
Yeshiva University, New York City

Associate Editor: Yaakov Elman
Assistant Professor of Judaic Studies
Yeshiva University, New York City

Moses Cordovero's Introduction to Kabbalah: An Annotated Translation of His *Or Ne'erav*

by

Ira Robinson

MYSU

The Michael Scharf Publication Trust
of the Yeshiva University Press
New York

Library of Congress Cataloging-in-Publication Data

Cordovero, Moses ben Jacob, 1522-1570.
[Pardes rimonim, English]
Moses Cordovero's introduction to Kabbalah : an annotated translation of his Or ne 'erav / by Ira Robinson.
p. cm.
Translation of Or ne 'erav, a popularization of Cordovero's Pardes rimonim.
Includes bibliographical references and index.
ISBN 0-88125-439-8
1. Cabala--Early works to 1800. I. Robinson, Ira, 1951-
II. Title.
BM525.C65413 1993
296.1'6--dc20 93-45501
CIP

Manufactured in the United States of America

This book is dedicated to the memory of my mother-in-law,

Mrs. Margaret Moskovitz

(1920—1988)

Her memory is a blessing.

Table of Contents

Acknowledgments

This work would not have seen the light of day but for the help and encouragement of numerous people. For them, these words will have to serve as a mere token repayment of a debt which can never truly be repaid.

My teachers, Isadore Twersky and Yosef Haim Yerushalmi, showed me how to read a medieval Jewish text and how to appreciate its significance. My colleagues in the Department of Religion, Concordia University, have provided me with a stimulating and challenging academic milieu in which I could grow. It is proverbially true that I learned most of all from my students. I would particularly like to thank Dr. Simcha Fishbane, presently at Touro College, for his many kindnesses and never-ending concern, and Mr. Michael Samuel, who verified a number of references for this volume.

I would like to acknowledge my debt to Rabbi Dr. Norman Lamm, editor of this series, and to the Michael Scharf Publication Trust of Yeshiva University for making possible the publication of this volume in the series "Sources and Studies in Kabbalah, Hasidism and Jewish Thought". My thanks also to the associate editor of the series, Dr. Yaakov Elman, and the rest of the staff at KTAV, for seeing this volume through all the many stages leading to its final publication.

Professor Elliot Wolfson, of New York University, read the manuscript and made a number of helpful suggestions which were adopted. The translator, obviously, is responsible for any errors which remain.

Mr. Brad Sabin-Hill, head of the Hebrew Section at the British Library, London, and previously curator of the Lowy Collection of Judaica in the National Library of Canada, Ottawa, graciously made available to me a photocopy of the first edition of *Or Ne'erav*, from which this translation was made.

Part of the material presented in the introduction to this work was originally published as an article in *Judaism*. I am grateful to the editors for permission to use that material here.

This translation had a long gestation. During its entire development, my wife, Sandra, and my children, Sara Libby and Yosef Dov, helped by being patient with me in my hours of distraction and by keeping me down to earth at times when I was getting lost in the realm of the sefirot.

My parents, Jacob and Hannah Robinson, are ultimately responsible for this work. My love of Judaism and of Jewish history was given me by them. This volume, while my work, is really theirs.

Montreal
November 7, 1991

Introduction

The Popularization of Kabbalah

In the late summer of 1587, Moses Cordovero's treatise *Or Ne'erav* ("The Pleasant Light") was published in Venice.[1] It was a book with several aims. First of all, it was written as a justification for the study of Kabbalah. As well, it contained detailed instructions for beginners on how to commence their Kabbalistic studies. Finally, it constituted an epitome of Cordovero's great systematic theology of Kabbalah entitled *Pardes Rimmonim* ("The Pomegranate Orchard"), which as yet remained in manuscript.[2] Taken as a whole, *Or Ne'erav* was clearly meant to serve as an elementary text for beginners in Kabbalah. It was also obviously intended as a means toward the popularization of a Judaic world-view which, at least at its inception, had been conceived as an esoteric interpretation of Torah, not meant for the ordinary person.

Historians of Judaism have long seen the sixteenth century as a pivotal period in the development of Kabbalah. The position maintained by Gershom Scholem, that prior to the sixteenth century Kabbalah belonged to relatively small groups of masters and their disciples, who had little desire to propagate their ideas among

1. It was published by "The House of Juan Di Gara." An annotation on the last page indicates that the typesetting was completed on the thirteenth of Av, 5347. On the publisher, see A. M. Haberman, *Ha-Madpis Juan di Gara u-Reshimat Sifrei Beyt Defuso*, ed. Y. Yudlov (Lod, 1982).

2. *Pardes Rimmonim* was first printed in Lublin in 1592.

the masses, has recently been challenged.[3] However, Scholem's emphasis on the centrality for Kabbalah of the sixteenth century, "with its programme of bringing its doctrines home to the community," retains its essential validity whether or not one also agrees that this program had as its ultimate purpose "preparing [the community] for the coming of the messiah."[4] In particular, Scholem's point that the ethical (*musar*) literature of Judaism prior to the sixteenth century shows little trace of Kabbalistic influence, whereas from the sixteenth century onward such works openly reflect the ethos of Kabbalah, is well taken.[5] The reservations expressed by Moshe Idel on important parts of Scholem's presentation of sixteenth-century Kabbalah have left this point unchallenged.[6]

Despite this recognition, the details of the change that was brought about in the position of Kabbalah in the sixteenth century among the broad masses of Jews have been relatively ignored by scholarship. This is at least in part because the concentration of most scholars of Kabbalah on what might be called the academic aspects of Kabbalistic thought has led to a situation in which the popularization of Kabbalah in the sixteenth century has been relatively ignored.[7] This book, which offers an annotated English translation of the treatise *Or Ne'erav*, seeks to shed light on the process by which the Kabbalah was to become the possession of every literate Jew.

3. Gershom Scholem, *Major Trends in Jewish Mysticism*, p. 244. Cf. Mark Verman, "Mysticism, Indoctrination and Society."

4. Scholem, *Major Trends*, p. 250.

5. Ibid., p. 251.

6. Idel, "One from a Town, Two from a Clan."

7. Exceptions to this rule include Louis Jacobs, *The Palm Tree of Deborah*, and Lawrence Fine, *Safed Spirituality*.

Kabbalah

The Hebrew term *kabbalah* refers to a body of knowledge "received" through a chain of transmission believed by rabbinic Jews to extend all the way back to the divine revelation at Sinai.[8] Rabbinic Judaism, the dominant interpretation of Judaism in the medieval and early modern era, assumed as an essential belief that this body of knowledge, called *torah* ("teaching"), encompassed two divisions—one written, the other oral. The written Torah consisted of the Pentateuch, while the oral Torah contained an authoritative interpretation of the laws and the narrative in the written Torah. Rabbinic Jews further believed that the oral Torah, which had been transmitted in unwritten form from master to disciple for well over a millennium, had begun to be reduced to writing in the form of the Mishnah, which was edited by Rabbi Judah the Patriarch in the second century C.E. The process was continued by the editing of other collections of rabbinic traditions, including the Tosefta, the Gemara in its Palestinian and Babylonian recensions, and numerous collections of midrashim.

The fact that these collections of traditions, designed to be transmitted orally, had been reduced to writing was of concern to rabbinic Jews. Their major conclusion was that the oral traditions had been written down in response to extraordinary circumstances endangering the survival of the oral Torah in its original form of transmission. Maimonides, in the introduction to his code of Judaic law, the *Mishneh Torah*, states the issue clearly:

> Why did our teacher [Rabbi Judah] the Patriarch [write down the Mishnah] and not leave matters as they were? [It was]

8. Cf. Mishnah, Avot 1:1.

> because he observed that the number of disciples was diminishing, fresh calamities were continually occurring, the wicked kingdom [of Rome] was extending its domain and increasing in power, and Israelites were wandering and emigrating to distant countries. Therefore he composed a work to serve as a handbook for all, the contents of which could be rapidly studied and not be forgotten.[9]

In other words, the writing down of the oral Torah was a response to a perceived threat to the "natural" transmission of the Torah. The writing of other rabbinic collections was seen in a similar light.[10]

It should not be thought, however, that the process of writing down the oral Torah meant that the oral Torah had ceased to exist. Indeed for most Jews there remained within the realm of Torah room for aspects of the Torah which had not been "published." These continued to be the exclusive province of oral transmission, or, if written, were written in such a way as to be virtually unintelligible and hence in need of oral reinforcement and explanation. Thus the Mishnah, in tractate Ḥagigah, refers to several aspects of Torah, including the sexual taboos (*'arayot*), the Account of Creation, and the Account of the Chariot, which were not to be expounded publicly.[11] The Torah, in other words, still held back certain secrets for oral transmission from master to disciple.

The notion that the Torah still had secrets to reveal became an extremely useful concept when, in the medieval period, Judaism—as well as Islam and Christianity—came into serious intellectual contact with the heritage of the science and philosophy of the ancient Greco-Roman world. For Jews, one of the major shifts

9. Maimonides, *Mishneh Torah*, introduction.

10. Ibid. It is noteworthy in this connection that Maimonides relates the writing of his halakhic compendium to his perception of a crisis in the transmission of Torah in his time.

11. Mishnah, Ḥagigah 2:1.

which ensued from this contact was the necessity of dealing with the numerous passages in the Hebrew Bible and rabbinic literature which presented God in anthropomorphic terms. By the twelfth and thirteenth centuries, the idea that the anthropomorphic passages in the Bible might be understood literally, while still sincerely believed by many Jews, had become severely problematic for Maimonides and others who took seriously the philosophical proofs for the incorporeality of God. Thus Maimonides equated with atheists, polytheists, and idolaters those who believed in one God but held that God possessed a body and an image.[12]

In order to deal with the implications of the seeming contradictions between the literal sense of the Bible and the findings of science, Maimonides and other medieval Jewish rationalists were compelled to assert that the Torah spoke "in human language"[13] concerning the deity and, therefore, that the words of the Torah, insofar as they indicated things which were "scientifically" impossible—such as attributing human bodily parts or emotions to God—were not to be taken literally but, rather, interpreted metaphorically.

The need to maintain a nonliteral interpretation of the Torah was widely felt among medieval Jewish intellectuals. However, the rationalist interpretations of Maimonides and others were not as widely accepted. In the first place, rationalistic philosophy was a discipline which was demonstrably non-Jewish in origin. Despite attempts to give it a Judaic pedigree,[14] the knowledge that philoso-

12. Maimonides, *Mishneh Torah*, Hilkhot Teshuvah 3:7. Cf. Rabad's animadversion to this statement, defending the "authenticity" of Jews who persist in anthropomorphic beliefs.

13. Cf. Marvin Fox, *Interpreting Maimonides: Studies in Methodology, Metaphysics and Moral Philosophy* (Chicago, 1990), p. 240.

14. Maimonides, *Guide of the Perplexed* 1.71. Cf. Isaac Husik, *A History of Mediaeval Jewish Philosophy* (New York, 1973), p. xvi.

phy was a foreign importation doubtless tended to lessen its acceptance. Secondly, and far more importantly, philosophy was hard pressed to explain the difference between the remote God of the philosophers, who had no interest in things that were not eternal, such as human beings, and the Biblical God, who played an active role in humankind's affairs and most particularly in those of His people, Israel. Furthermore, Jewish philosophers often found it hard to explain satisfactorily the details of the legislation in the Torah. Maimonides' historical explanations of such things as the prohibition of mingling linen and woolen threads (*sha'atnez*) may have satisfied some, but doubtless left others wondering whether such formulations did not tend to relativize the Torah's commandments and potentially threaten the continued observance of Torah law.[15]

In contrast with this, Kabbalah offered its adherents a means whereby the Torah in its entirety could be satisfactorily explained in a nonliteralist manner. The details of the commandments no less than their general principles could be understood by referring to Kabbalistic doctrines.[16] Moreover, care was taken to present the ideas of Kabbalah in such a way as to ensure that they would appear to be entirely intrinsic to the rabbinic tradition. Thus the first major Kabbalistic work, *Sefer ha-Bahir*,[17] as well as Kabbalah's

15. Cf. Ira Robinson, "Halakha, Kabbala and Philosophy in the Thought of Joseph Jabez," p. 393.

16. On the Kabbalistic interpretation of the commandments, see Daniel Matt, "The Mystic and the Mizvot," and Elliot Wolfson, "Mystical Rationalization of the Commandments in *Sefer ha-Rimmon*," pp. 222, 249-251.

17. On the Midrashic nature of the *Bahir*, see Gershom Scholem, *Origins of the Kabbalah*, pp. 39-44, 49-53, and Joseph Dan, "Midrash and the Dawn of Kabbalah," pp. 127-139.

major thirteenth-century exposition, the Zohar,[18] presented themselves as Midrashic expositions of the Torah—in other words, as works in a classical genre.

Kabbalah, which first emerged into the light of day in twelfth-century Provence, and which received its classical statement in the Zohar, in thirteenth-century Spain,[19] understood God's relationship with the created universe in the following way.

God, in His most fundamental reality, is unknown to man and, in principle, unknowable. The only thing known about God in this fundamental reality is His existence. Kabbalists called the God of this fundamental reality Eyn Sof, meaning "without limit," or even 'Ayin ("nothingness"), signifying that from the perspective of mankind, there was "nothing" that one could know about Him.

Eyn Sof initiated a process which the Kabbalists called Aẓilut ("emanation"), which eventuated in a system of ten sefirot. The sefirot, taken as a whole, represented God as experienced by human beings. The following is a somewhat simplified depiction of the process. The first sefirah to be emanated, called Keter ("crown"), marked the transition point between Eyn Sof and the sefirotic system. The next two sefirot, Ḥokhmah ("wisdom") and Binah ("understanding"), represented a male and a female principle, respectively. Ḥokhmah and Binah, in union, produced the seven other sefirot, Gedulah ("greatness") or Raḥamim ("mercy"), Gevurah ("might"), Tiferet ("glory"), Neẓaḥ ("triumph"), Hod ("splendor"), Yesod ("foundation"), and Malkhut ("kingdom"). The three upper sefirot, Keter, Ḥokhmah, and Binah, were considered relatively less accessible to the human mind than the lower seven,

18. On the Zohar's Midrashic approach, see Itamar Gruenwald, "From Talmudic to Zoharic Hermeneutics."

19. On the Zohar, see Scholem, *Major Trends*, pp. 156-243; Daniel Matt, *Zohar*, introduction; and Yehuda Liebes, "How the Zohar Was Written."

which were taken to represent the sometimes diametrically opposed qualities attributed to God in the Hebrew Bible and the rabbinic literature. Thus God the Merciful was seen as represented by the sefirah Gedulah. God's attribute of stern justice was embodied in the sefirah Gevurah. Tiferet was the synthesis between mercy and justice.

Though the Kabbalists asserted that all of the sefirot were interrelated and, indeed, that all were One, nonetheless they tended to concentrate their attention on the relationship between two sefirot in particular: Tiferet and Malkhut. Tiferet was seen as the central sefirah and a male principle. Ideally, it was to enter into union with Malkhut, a female principle which marked the point of transition between the realm of the sefirot and the created universe. Through the union of Tiferet and Malkhut flowed the divine energy which created and sustained the universe. When the Tiferet-Malkhut union was consummated, the flow of divine energy was unabated. When the union was interrupted, however, the flow of divine energy ceased sustaining the universe and, instead, served to strengthen the forces of cosmic evil, referred to as the "Other Side" (Sitra A"ra), and conceived as arrayed in a counter-sefirotic structure.

Where Kabbalists found themselves divided was on the question of whether the sefirot, taken as a whole, constituted an "instrument" employed by God for His revelation to His creatures or whether, in fact, the sefirotic realm *was* God.

Within this divine economy, human beings, and especially the Jews, were not mere passive observers. Kabbalists held that Jews, through their performance of the commandments of the Torah and through their prayers, could influence the sefirotic realm. Prayer and Torah observance, undertaken with the correct intention, would align the sefirot correctly and help accomplish the union of Tiferet and Malkhut. Sin, on the other hand, served to disrupt the harmony of the sefirot, sunder the sefirotic union, and render aid and comfort to the evil forces of the Other Side.

The responsibility of the individual Jew for the well-being of the cosmos was coupled with a belief that events and actions in the human sphere indicated corresponding processes in the sefirotic realm. Thus each earthly action had its sefirotic counterpart. For the Kabbalist, this meant that literally everything was to be related to the divine and was to be understood in a sense beyond its surface meaning.

For its adherents, Kabbalah was clearly a tool of great power and sophistication with which to understand the universe. It was just as clearly the ultimate secret of the Torah. This being so, it was by no means clear whether this secret doctrine was to be publicized to wider circles or not.

Those who wished to teach Kabbalistic doctrines, and, in particular, those who desired to reach a mass audience, were faced with a seemingly unsolvable problem. They were fully convinced that their discipline was none other than *Ma'aseh Merkavah*, the esoteric lore referred to in the Mishnah. Thus they were seemingly bound by the Mishnah's prohibition against expounding this material "before even one student."[20]

In this spirit, one of the first major Kabbalistic masters in twelfth-century Provence, Isaac the Blind, went on record in a letter to Spain against the indiscriminate spread of Kabbalah through public exposition and the composition of Kabbalistic treatises that might fall into the "wrong" hands. His remarks were addressed to circles of students of Kabbalah in Spain who were composing Kabbalistic treatises and even, like Naḥmanides, incorporating

20. Cf. n. 11 above.

Kabbalistic indications in a commentary on the Torah meant for the general public.[21]

Those Kabbalists, from the thirteenth through the fifteenth century, who did engage in the writing of Kabbalistic works, generally did so in full consciousness of the fact that they were addressing audiences whose members could not all be trusted with the secrets of the Torah which they were purveying. For this reason they often sought to conceal as well as reveal, in order to make sure that oral direction would still be needed in addition to the written treatises. Thus Abraham ben Eliezer Halevi, a Kabbalist of the generation of the Spanish Expulsion, asserted in one of his works that Kabbalistic authors invariably omitted certain elements from their writings in order to maintain the need for the Kabbalah to be transmitted orally.[22] Given this approach, one can easily appreciate the extent to which those desiring to popularize Kabbalah had to overcome an ingrained opposition to its widespread dissemination even on the part of Kabbalists, let alone opponents of the discipline. This fact, in addition to the painstaking effort, mentioned earlier, to present the Kabbalah as wholly intrinsic to the Judaic tradition, went a long way toward reducing the expressed opposition to Kabbalah to relatively minor proportions. There were, indeed, Jews who objected vigorously to Kabbalah, for instance on the grounds that the tenfold character of the sefirot could not be reconciled with God's absolute unity. Apparently,

21. Scholem, *Origins of the Kabbalah*, pp. 393-394. On Nahmanides' Kabbalistic doctrines, see Moshe Idel, "We Have No Tradition on This," and Elliot Wolfson, "By Way of Truth."

22. Ira Robinson, "Abraham Ben Eliezer Halevi," p. 198, nn. 21-23. For a similar warning on the inherent danger of delving into the mysteries of Kabbalah without a master and relying solely on what is written in books, see Naḥmanides, *Derush 'al Kohelet*, in *Kitve ha-Ramban*, ed. C. Chavel (Jerusalem, Mossad ha-Rav Kook, 1963), vol. 1, p. 180.

however, these objections were relatively few, perhaps consonant with the limited distribution of Kabbalah within Jewry.[23]

It is thus reasonably clear that the process whereby Kabbalah came to the attention of the Jewish public in its first centuries was slow, halting, and somewhat ambivalent.

This situation began to change in the sixteenth century. In the aftermath of the expulsion from the Iberian peninsula in the 1490s, an upheaval which had the same sort of resonance for Jews of that generation as the Holocaust has for ours, Kabbalah began going public in a big way. Kabbalistic works like the Zohar began to be printed, amid a major controversy regarding the propriety of printing them.[24]

More importantly, systematic treatises on Kabbalah began to appear. One of these comprehensive guides to Kabbalah was written by the aforementioned Abraham ben Eliezer Halevi. Entitled *Massoret ha-Ḥokhmah* ("Tradition of Wisdom"), it was a defense of the discipline of Kabbalah against its detractors, a condemnation of opposing Kabbalistic schools, and a praise of the benefits deriving from the study of Kabbalah. However, the exposition of Kabbalistic doctrine in this work is brief and sketchy in the extreme.[25] Similar to Halevi's work in scope, but somewhat more well known, because printed, is Judah Ḥayyat's introduction to his commentary on *Ma'arekhet ha-Elohut* ("The System of Divinity").[26] On a much grander scale is the work of another contemporary, Meir ibn Gabbai, whose exposition of Kabbalah was entitled

23. Cf. Idel, *Kabbalah*, p. 3.

24. Isaiah Tishby, "Ha-Pulmus 'al *Sefer ha-Zohar* be-Me'ah ha-Shesh Esreh be-Italiyah."

25. Robinson, "Abraham ben Eliezer Halevi," pp. 195-200.

26. Judah Ḥayyat, commentary on *Ma'arekhet ha-Elohut* (Mantua, 1558), introduction.

'Avodat ha-Kodesh ("The Holy Service"). Scholem characterized it as "perhaps the finest account of Kabbalistic speculation before the resurgence of the Kabbalah in Safed."[27]

Safed

Most importantly, broad sections of the Jewish public began assimilating the Kabbalistic ethos into their own lives. Nowhere was this process more apparent than in the town of Safed, in the Galilee. After the Ottoman conquest of the Land of Israel in 1517, Safed attracted a large number of Jewish immigrants, largely from among the Spanish and Portuguese exiles and their children. These people settled in the Land of Israel partly because they sought to be in the place where they expected an imminent messianic redemption and partly because it was part of the burgeoning Ottoman Empire, to which many Jews were attracted at this time.[28]

In Safed, many attempts were made to prepare for the expected redemption. Among them were controversial projects like the attempt, in the 1530s, to reintroduce an authentic rabbinic ordination,[29] as well as a mass movement for repentance and for observance of the commandments of the Torah which, so our sources inform us, attracted thousands of followers.[30]

Kabbalah was an integral part of the Safed ethos, and the town became a center for the study and dissemination of Kabbalah

27. Scholem, *Kabbalah*, p. 69. Cf. Roland Goetschel, *Meir Ibn Gabbay.*

28. Cf. Yiẓḥak Ben Ẓvi, "Eretz Yisrael Under Ottoman Rule," in *The Jews: Their History*, ed. Louis Finkelstein (New York, 1972), pp. 406 ff.

29. Jacob Katz, "Maḥloket ha-Semikhah beyn Rabbi Yaakov Berab veha-Ralbaḥ."

30. Ronit Meroz, *Redemption in the Lurianic Teaching*, p. 3.

without parallel in history. The number of Kabbalists who were concentrated in Safed was relatively sizable. But beyond their actual numbers, they were able to decisively influence the community at large in unprecedented ways. Several liturgical innovations, such as the preliminary service on the eve of the Sabbath (*kabbalat shabbat*) and the midnight penitential service (*tikkun ḥaẓẓot*) emanated from these circles and were accepted by Jews throughout the world.[31]

The influence of the Kabbalists and their teachings on the life of the ordinary Jew did not happen accidentally. The Kabbalists had made a decision to involve the community at large in their discipline.[32] A good part of their motivation for doing so stemmed, doubtless, from the assumption that they were living in the age immediately preceding the messianic redemption. Of this age, the *Ra'aya Mehemna* had said: "Israel will come to taste of the tree of life which is this book of Zohar. With it they will go out of the Exile with [divine] mercy."[33]

A clear implication of this assumption was that now, as never before, there was an obligation to make public the secrets of Kabbalah which had heretofore remained hidden. The most prominent of the Safed Kabbalists to feel this way was Moses Cordovero. *Or Ne'erav* is one of the major means by which he expressed this imperative.

31. Cf. Fine, *Safed Spirituality*, introduction.

32. Meroz points out that this decision was one characteristic of Cordovero and his school but uncharacteristic of Isaac Luria and his disciples. *Redemption in the Lurianic Teaching*, pp. 4-5.

33. *Ra'aya Mehemna*, Zohar III, 124b. Cordovero expected the messianic advent in the period between 1540 and 1589. Cf. Beracha Zak, "Galut Yisrael ve-Galut ha-Shekhinah be-*Or Yakar* le-Rabbi Mosheh Cordovero."

Moses Cordovero

Cordovero was born in the year 1522 and settled in Safed as a young man.[34] His teacher of rabbinics was none other than R. Joseph Karo, author of the standard systematization of Halakhah, the *Shulḥan Arukh*.[35] At the age of twenty Cordovero began his Kabḅalistic studies under Solomon ha-Levi Alkabetz, whose sister he subsequently married.[36] He studied, taught, and wrote in Safed until his death in 1570, at the age of forty-eight.

There is a sense in which Cordovero was following the same path in Kabbalah that his master, Karo, had followed in Halakhah. Both were systematizers. Cordovero sought to do nothing less than synthesize a systematic Kabbalistic theology from the exegetical teachings of the Zohar just as Karo had attempted to create a clear methodology for the determination of Jewish law out of the myriad works and opinions of his predecessors.

Cordovero had worked out this systematic theology by the age of twenty-seven in a work he entitled *Pardes Rimmonim* ("The Pomegranate Garden"). It eclipsed all previous efforts to systematize Kabbalah. In this work, he set forth a comprehensive Kabbalistic account of God, man, and creation that was to become a standard account of the field.[37] If Cordovero has been called the greatest theoretician of Kabbalah, it is mostly due to the *Pardes Rimmonim*. Indeed, given that the bulk of Cordovero's writings remained in manuscript for centuries after his death, his vast reputation largely

34. On Cordovero and his thought, see Yosef Ben-Shlomo, *The Mystical Theology of Moses Cordovero*, esp. chap. 1. For a summary in English, see his *Encyclopaedia Judaica* article on Cordovero, vol. 5, cols. 967-970.

35. On Karo, see R. J. Z. Werblowsky, *Joseph Karo*.

36. On Alkabetz, see Beracha Zak, "Torat ha-Sod shel R. Shelomoh Alkabetz."

37. Cf. Scholem, *Major Trends*, p. 252.

depends on this work.[38] *Pardes Rimmonim* was not, however, entirely easy of access. It was designed for those who already had a fairly strong background in Kabbalah and its texts. Indeed Cordovero recognized that Kabbalistic novices who read *Pardes Rimmonim* would be likely to do themselves more harm than good.[39] It was thus inadequate as a tool with which to attract new adherents to his Kabbalistic ideology and to refute the counter-claims of opponents of Kabbalah and of rival schools of Kabbalistic interpretation.

What, then, of these others? What of those who were interested in the subject but had never approached it and would be lost in its complexities? What of those who, having heard of the subject, were hesitant, not knowing whether they could or should engage in its study? The messianic imperative, which affected Cordovero no less than other Jews of his generation,[40] indicated that Kabbalah had to be popularized if its knowledge was to spread among the people in order to hasten the Messiah's coming. For this reason, among others, Cordovero determined to embody the Kabbalah's teachings in a form accessible to readers who were not specialists in Kabbalistic studies.

One such venture was an ethical treatise which he titled *Tomer Devorah* ("The Palm Tree of Deborah").[41] In it, Cordovero successfully integrated the genre of moral and ethical exhortation, which was fairly widely accepted, with Kabbalistic teachings concerning the sefirot. Thus the exhortation to internalize the qualities of God,

38. Thus his *Elimah Rabbati* was not published until 1881. *Shiur Komah* was published in 1883. His extensive commentary on the Zohar, *Or Yakar*, began its publication in the 1960s and is still incomplete.

39. Cordovero, *Pardes Rimmonim*, introduction.

40. See Beracha Zak, "Sheloshah Zemanei Geulah be-*Or Yakar* le-Rabbi Mosheh Cordovero."

41. See Jacobs, *Palm Tree of Deborah*, introduction.

such as mercy and lovingkindness, was imbued with the tenfold division of the sefirot such that each sefirah encompassed a moral and ethical principle which Jews were exhorted to make a part of their lives. This work, which was the first of its kind, was followed by numerous others in the sixteenth, seventeenth, and eighteenth centuries.[42]

Or Ne'erav

The other major attempt by Cordovero to popularize his Kabbalistic teaching was the treatise translated here, *Or Ne'erav*. Because it contains no introduction by the author, we are unable to say with any certainty when it was written or why. From its contents, however, we can readily discern that Cordovero utilized his immense intellectual and pedagogical talents to create a work with a dual purpose. As his son, Gedaliah, who brought the book to press, indicates in his introduction, he abridged the material which was argued *in extenso* in *Pardes Rimmonim*. To this abridgement he added, at the beginning of the treatise, "additional chapters . . . to [cause others to] understand and to teach the usefulness of this discipline and the necessity for learning it."[43] Thus, on the one hand, *Or Ne'erav* served as an argument for the legitimacy of Kabbalah and its study. On the other hand, it presented an epitome of *Pardes Rimmonim* suitable for people just beginning their Kabbalistic studies.

We will have something to say regarding this latter aspect of *Or Ne'erav* later on. At present, however, we are interested precisely in

42. Cf. Joseph Dan, *Jewish Mysticism and Jewish Ethics*.
43. *Or Ne'erav*, p. 3a.

the "additional chapters" which come at the beginning. They give us an important insight into the way in which a major Kabbalistic scholar envisaged the study of Kabbalah by beginners at the very time when Kabbalah was emerging to compete openly for a place in the Jewish curriculum.[44]

With regard to the first purpose of the treatise, that of establishing Kabbalah's legitimacy as an intellectual discipline, it might be said that Cordovero basically continued the genre of "defenses" of true Kabbalah against its detractors and opponents both within and without the Kabbalist camp.[45] His treatment of his sources is unmistakably Cordoveran in its thoroughness and meticulousness but is nonetheless not terribly original. Indeed, it might even be said that some of the groups Cordovero argued against, such as those who entirely denied that the Torah could be interpreted esoterically, did not constitute a formal school of thought in his day and were included only in order to fill the spectrum of logical possibilities of opposition to his enterprise.[46] What is new in *Or Ne'erav* is Cordovero's detailed vision of the ideal Kabbalistic education.

For Cordovero, the ideal student should have attained the age of twenty before commencing his study of Kabbalah. In stating this, he placed himself in conscious opposition to the view that Kabbalistic studies should be limited to those who had achieved

44. On the competition for a place in the Jewish curriculum, see Ira Robinson, "Torah and Halakha in Medieval Judaism," *Studies in Religion* 13 (1984): 47-55.

45. Cf. Judah Ḥayyat's introduction to his commentary on *Ma'arekhet ha-Elohut*. Ḥayyat's treatment of this subject, though briefer than Cordovero's, shows a number of interesting parallels with *Or Ne'erav*.

46. Cf. n. 20 above. If, indeed, little opposition to Kabbalah is documented in this era, the logical possibilities are that Cordovero is either arguing against real points of view that have not come down to us or is simply presenting the potential Kabbalist with a refutation of all possible objections to Kabbalah.

the age of "understanding"—forty.[47] Though Cordovero does not mention it in this context, he asserts in the introduction to *Pardes Rimmonim* that his own education in Kabbalah began at the age of twenty. Thus, in a self-reference, he could emphatically state: "Many have acted in accordance with our opinion and succeeded."[48]

Cordovero's own experience with the study of Kabbalah is likely to have inspired him to demand of the potential student that he "first strip from himself the shell of gross pride which prevents him from attaining the truth. He should [then] direct his heart to heaven [to pray] that he not fail."[49] In the introduction to *Pardes Rimmonim*, Cordovero claimed to have undergone a similar conversion experience at the age of twenty, in which he renounced worldly vanities and turned to Kabbalah. As he said of himself, at the age of twenty "My Creator aroused me as one who is aroused from sleep, and I said to my soul, 'Until when will you cause the misbehaving daughter to disappear?'"[50]

The student, having attained the requisite age and deportment, should also have undergone a rigorous preparatory course in the classic exoteric Jewish texts. Influenced here as elsewhere by Maimonides, Cordovero asserted that the ideal curriculum ought to be divided into three divisions: Scripture, Mishnah, and Talmud.[51] Mishnah was defined as the entire range of rabbinic law, while Talmud was meant to refer to *pardes* (esoteric studies). Thus Cordovero stated:

47. Cf. Mishnah, Avot 5:21. Cf. also Idel, "On the History of the Interdiction Against the Study of Kabbalah Before the Age of Forty."

48. *Or Ne'erav*, p. 19b; cf. p. 17a.

49. Ibid., p. 19b.

50. Cordovero, *Pardes Rimmonim*, introduction.

51. Cf. Maimonides, *Mishneh Torah*, Hilkhot Talmud Torah 1:11-12.

> He [the prospective student] must be accustomed to engaging in profound *pilpul* [dialectical reasoning] so that he might be accustomed and able to strip [relevant] matters from parables. . . . He must apply himself to fill his belly with [the study of] the laws of the Gemara and the explanation of the commandments on the literal level in the work of Rabbi Moses ben Maimon, the *Yad*. . . . He should also guide himself in the study of Scripture—whether [it be] much or little. . . . [Then] he will not fail.[52]

Of course, mastery of these preparatory subjects should not become so complete as to inordinately delay the study of Kabbalah. As Cordovero stated:

> There are those who imagine that before pursuing [Kabbalah], they must first master the science of astronomy. They have other notions which keep them from following the straight path. They sanctimoniously give themselves the excuse that their bellies are not yet full of the bread and meat of the Gemara. For these poor people, their entire lives will not be sufficient to learn even a bit of [Gemara], let alone to fill their bellies so that they could partake of this science [of Kabbalah] and be sated. Thus the poor people go to their eternal rest bereft of wisdom.[53]
>
> Beyond proper preparatory study, would-be students of Kabbalah must also possess a strong desire to study the subject for its own sake in order to enter into its mysteries, to know their Master and to achieve a wondrous level in the true acquisition of knowledge of the Torah. To pray before their Master and to unify, through His commandments, the Holy One, blessed be He, and His Shekhinah.[54]

52. *Or Ne'erav*, p. 19b. On *pilpul* as a Cordoveran concept, see Ben Shlomo, *Mystical Theology*, p. 29.

53. *Or Ne'erav*, p. 11a.

54. Ibid., p. 17a.

By way of contrast, those who desire to study Kabbalah merely as one discipline among many, and for whom acquiring "a bit of this science is the same . . . as [acquiring] a smattering of medicine, astronomy, logic, mathematics, and the other sciences,"[55] were characterized as sinners.

So much for the student of Kabbalah; what must one expect of the teacher of this subject? Cordovero asserted that a student who truly desires to study Kabbalah should take as a teacher someone who has fulfilled the requisite standards for a Kabbalist. Thus, a teacher of Kabbalah must be a person with an adequate background in the exoteric texts, who has mastered Kabbalah for its own sake and not as one discipline among many. To study with a teacher who does not fulfill these conditions will lead the student to error and might eventually result in his losing his faith.[56]

However, what is one to do if one is unable to find a suitable teacher? Does the lack of a qualified teacher mean that one may not begin the study of Kabbalah at all? Cordovero's answer to this problem is self-study. Doing it by yourself, though it may lead you to error, is preferable to refraining from any attempt to study Kabbalah. In the end, Cordovero asserted, even the erroneous study of Kabbalah has its divine reward.[57] In an era in which teachers of Kabbalah were few and manuscripts of Kabbalistic texts were scattered, it is not unlikely that Cordovero's accommodating attitude toward self-study reflected the contemporary situation.

Just as Cordovero was exacting with regard to the choice of an instructor, preferring self-study to instruction by an inadequate teacher, so was he exacting with regard to the texts the student should study. Living in an era in which several more or less

55. Ibid., pp. 16b-17a.
56. Ibid., p. 23a.
57. Ibid., pp. 15a-b.

systematic accounts of Kabbalah were available, Cordovero advised the beginning student to avoid all of them. The authors of these Kabbalistic works, he said, had "compose[ed] their books in riddles and metaphors so that their message is encumbered by much [extraneous] matter. We ourselves would not do this, God forbid. It is improper to place a blemish upon sanctified things."[58]

Rather than rely upon such books, Cordovero urged students to concentrate mainly on the Zoharic literature and such sanctified works as *Sefer Yeẓirah* ("Book of Creation") and *Sefer ha-Bahir* ("Book of Clear Light").

> [The student] should stick to these books lovingly. He will succeed in [mastering] this science on condition that he delve deeply into them and [devote to them] exceptional study. He will then find explanations for most of what is to be found in the books of the latter commentators, which he need not consult. It is not our intention to declare these [latter works] unfit, God forbid, but rather to indicate to the student the path which is short, though it seems to be long.[59]

In pursuing the study of these texts, some times are better for learning than others.

> It is certainly easy for a student to study throughout the day. However, the optimum time for gaining profound wisdom is the long night, from midnight on, or on the Sabbath day, which is [itself] a factor. This [also applies to] the eve of the Sabbath, commencing at noontime and on holidays, particularly on Aẓeret [Shavuot]. I have tried this many times and

58. Ibid., p. 21b. By contrast, Judah Ḥayyat does recommend Kabbalistic treatises, including those of Naḥmanides, Joseph Gikatilla, and Menaḥem Recanati. See the introduction to his commentary on *Ma'arekhet ha-Elohut*, p. 3b.

59. *Or Ne'erav*, pp. 21b-22a.

found it to be a marvelously successful day. Also, there is great success [in studying] on Sukkot in the sukkah. These times [I have] mentioned I have tried. I am speaking from experience.[60]

In addition to studying the optimum texts at the optimum times, the student was to approach his studies in the following way:

First of all, [the student] should review the texts many times, making notes in order to remember his studies fluently. He should not delve too deeply at first. Secondly, he should study the material with great concentration according to his ability. . . . At times [the amount of time given to] the two forms of study should be increased and sometimes lessened, all according to the need of the hour and the [degree of] peace of mind. . . . Though it may seem to the student that he does not understand [the texts], he should nevertheless not cease studying, for his Master will faithfully cause him to discover esoteric wisdom. . . . I have experienced this innumerable times. . . . Should any subject in this science seem doubtful for [the student], he should wait. For in the course of time the matter will be revealed to him. The essential reward [for the study] of this science is [derived from] waiting for [the revelation of] the mysteries which will be revealed to him in the course of time.[61]

As previously noted, Moses Cordovero's son, Gedaliah, considered all the material we have dealt with so far as merely prefatory to the essential part of *Or Ne'erav*, which is the epitome of *Pardes Rimmonim*. The section of the work containing the epitome is entitled "On the Necessary Preparations for Beginners in This Science."[62] We noted earlier that Cordovero, in criticizing the au-

60. Ibid., p. 19b. On the concept of midnight in the practice of Safed Kabbalists, see Fine, *Safed Spirituality*, pp. 17-18.

61. *Or Ne'erav*, pp. 22a, 32b-33a.

62. Ibid., pp. 33b ff.

thors of other Kabbalistic treatises, stated that his work would differ from theirs. He was presumably saying, though not in so many words, that *Pardes Rimmonim was* an adequate text for Kabbalistic studies and that *Or Ne'erav* was a proper way for beginners to be introduced to the material it contained.

It has been observed that Cordovero's ethical work, *Tomer Devorah*, pioneered a genre in which Kabbalistic ideas and motifs began suffusing and controlling moral and ethical discourse.[63] It has not been sufficiently noted, however, that *Or Ne'erav* begins another trend: the publication of abridgements and epitomes of Kabbalistic works. In the seventeenth century, two further abridgements of *Pardes Rimmonim* appeared.[64] In addition, *Reshit Ḥokhmah* ("Beginning of Wisdom") by Moses Cordovero's disciple, Elijah De Vidas, who saw his work as a sort of primer leading to the study of *Pardes Rimmonim*, was issued in abridged form.[65] Other Kabbalistic works, such as Isaiah Hurwitz's *Shnei Luḥot ha-Berit* ("The Two Tablets of the Covenant") also generated abridgements.[66]

In any account of the attempt to popularize the study of Kabbalah, Moses Cordovero and his *Or Ne'erav* deserve a prominent place. However, this is not because the work attained a continuing degree of popularity. It was never completely forgotten amid the welter of books offering an entree to the study of Kabbalah and was reprinted several times.[67] Nonetheless, due

63. Cf. n. 37 above.

64. Menaḥem Azariah of Fano, *Pelaḥ ha-Rimmon* (1600) and Samuel Gallico, *Assis Rimmonim* (1601).

65. Fine, *Safed Spirituality*, p. 181. Cf. Mordecai Pachter, "Elijah De Vidas' *Beginning of Wisdom* and Its Abbreviated Versions," and Zev Gries, "Iẓẓuv Safrut ha-Hanhagot ha-Ivrit be-Me'ah ha-Shesh Esreh uva-Me'ah ha-Shva Esreh u-Mashmauto ha-Historit."

66. Yeḥiel Michel Epstein, *Kiẓẓur Shla* (Fuerth, 1693).

67. See Ḥayyim Dov Friedberg, *Bet Eked Sefarim* (Tel-Aviv, 1956), vol. 1, p. 51.

partly, perhaps, to its admittedly unfinished character,[68] and partly to the relative eclipse of Cordoveran Kabbalah by the writings of Isaac Luria and his disciples,[69] it never became the important conduit to the study of Kabbalah that it was intended to be. It remains, however, a precious document for historians of Kabbalah and of Jewish education, for it enables us to gain an insight into what a major authority on Kabbalah thought about Kabbalistic education in an era in which that education—like Kabbalah itself—was undergoing tremendous expansion and change.

On the Translation

This translation of *Or Ne'erav* was prepared on the basis of the first edition (Venice, 1587), the pagination of which is indicated in the text with brackets. The introductory material that prefaced the first edition will be found in the appendices. The text was compared with later editions, particularly that edited by Rabbi Yehuda Zvi Brandwein (Tel-Aviv, 1965), whose notes were often helpful.

Care was taken to render the Hebrew and Aramaic text into a readable English. In order to facilitate this goal, words and phrases not contained in the original, which were considered necessary aids to comprehension, were added in brackets. Quotations from Scripture are printed in italics. In many cases Cordovero did not quote complete phrases or verses; when the omission is at the beginning or end of a quotation this is self-evident, when it occurs in the middle an ellipsis (. . .) is utilized to indicate that something is missing. No part of Cordovero's text was omitted from the translation.

68. The clearest indication of this is that Cordovero did not provide an introduction to the work.

69. See Meroz, *Redemption in the Lurianic Teaching*, chap. 1.

[6b]

PART I

On the Rectification of the Harm Incurred on Account of the Opinions of Those Who Stay Aloof from This Science

1

Those who shun this science[1] [of Kabbalah] can be divided into three classes. The first [class comprises] those who shun it because they think that there is no need to believe [in the existence] of an esoteric meaning of Torah. There are a number of reasons [for their opinion]. Some believe that the words [of the Torah] must be understood literally. Hence they have no desire [to comprehend] the esoteric. Who, indeed, can force them to believe in the ten sefirot[2] and the other aspects of this science?

Furthermore, they have no desire to transcend their belief in [God's] wondrous unity.[3] When some aspect of this discipline

1. Cordovero consistently refers to Kabbalah as *ḥokhmah*, the word medieval Jews used for "science," as in *ḥokhmat ha-refuah*, the "science of medicine." It was Cordovero's conviction, and that of some of his contemporaries, that Kabbalah could provide a "scientific" key by means of which it would be possible to understand the secrets of the universe. See David Ruderman, *Kabbalah, Magic and Science: The Cultural Universe of a Sixteenth Century Jewish Physician* (Cambridge: Harvard University Press, 1988), p. 139. Though I have translated *ḥokhmah* as "science," it should be understood in the sense of "knowledge." An alternative translation would be "gnosis."

2. Kabbalists believe that God, insofar as He can be perceived by human beings, is to be comprehended as a dynamic system of ten sefirot, which are emanated from a source, Eyn Sof, which is utterly beyond human comprehension. For a description of this system, see Daniel Matt, *Zohar: the Book of Enlightenment* (New York: Paulist Press, 1983), pp. 33-37.

3. Professor Elliot Wolfson has pointed out to me in a personal communication that the reference at this point might be to philosophers who reject the doctrine of the sefirot because they do not wish to transcend their belief in God's wondrous unity. Isaac of Acre, a thirteenth-century Kabbalist, made a similar critique of the philosophers.

comes before them, whether it concerns Eyn Sof[4] or the form of the Torah,[5] they begin to denounce the enlightened [Kabbalists], who appear to them as little short of heretics.[6] Some of them take up this argument—to the deficiency of their souls—without believing it entirely. Others sincerely believe it to be true. To argue against such people is nearly forbidden because of the embitterment [it causes]. Nonetheless the honor of the Torah must be upheld and this opinion must be refuted.

Without doubt it is concerning these men and their like that King Solomon, peace upon him, said, *The fool does not desire understanding, but only to air his thoughts* (Prov. 18:2). It is apparent that one who follows his desires and spurns enlightenment in the mysteries of the Torah[7] can be called a fool, since he continues his folly and his intoxication with this lowly world. [7a] [The verse] states, *The fool does not desire understanding*—these are the esoteric subjects hidden within the exoteric matter. This definition of understanding is the one which [the sages], their memory be a blessing, [used when they] said, "He who understands one thing from another."[8]

The fool, then, has no desire [to comprehend] the hidden things which require understanding to discover. Thus [Solomon]

4. Eyn Sof (lit. "Without End") is what Kabbalists call God in His aspect prior to the emanation and beyond human comprehension.

5. *Ẓurat ha-torah.* On this concept, see Gershom Scholem, "The Meaning of the Torah in Jewish Mysticism," in his *On the Kabbalah and Its Symbolism* (New York: Schocken, 1969), pp. 32-86.

6. Though little now remains of it, there apparently existed a large literature denouncing Kabbalah as heresy. Such denunciations seem to have been the impetus for Cordovero's remarks here. See Moshe Idel, *Kabbalah: New Perspectives* (New Haven: Yale University Press, 1988), pp. 1-2.

7. Kabbalah was believed by its adherents to be the repository of the mysteries of the Torah.

8. Ḥagigah 14a. The context of this statement in Ḥagigah has reference to knowledge of esoteric doctrines.

said, *A man of understanding can draw them out* (Prov. 20:5).[9] [The fool] only [desires] *to air his thoughts* [with regard to] the revealed matters which serve as a garment [concealing] the esoteric aspects and which appear to constitute the plain meaning of the subject.[10] These matters are indeed revealed to the heart, but they are not [revealed] to the hearts of the enlightened—only to the hearts of fools like him. This is the meaning of *to air his thoughts*: It refers to his limited mental capacity.

Of these men and their like, Rabbi Simeon bar Yoḥai, peace upon him, said in the *Tikkunim* [no. 43]:[11]

> *In the beginning* (Gen. 1:1).
>
> There it is dry, and here *the river dries up and is parched* (Job14:11).
>
> At that time when he is dry and she is dry, sons cry out below in unification and say, *Hear, O Israel* (Deut. 6:4).
>
> And there is *no voice in response* (I Kings 18:26).
>
> Thus it is written, *Then they will call to Me, and I will not answer* (Prov. 1:28).
>
> This concerns one who removes Kabbalah and wisdom from the oral Torah and the written Torah, who causes that they should not attempt [to acquire] them, and who asserts that there is nothing beyond the plain meaning of the Torah and the Talmud.

9. The Masoretic text of the Bible reads *tevunah* (singular), whereas Cordovero wrote *tevunot* (plural). This inaccuracy is probably the result of his citing the verse from memory.

10. The Zohar III, 152a, reacts furiously against such people. Cordovero cites this passage *in extenso* in pt. I, chap. 2.

11. P. 82a. *Tikkunei Zohar* is a collection of Zoharic writings which constitute a commentary to the portion *Bereshit*. See Gershom Scholem, *Kabbalah* (New York: Quadrangle, 1974), pp. 218-219.

Certainly it is as if he removed the flow from that river and that garden.[12]
Woe to him.
It were better for him had he never been created in the world, and had he never taught the written Torah and oral Torah, for it is considered as if he had returned the world to *formlessness and void* (Gen. 1:2) and bequeathed poverty and length of exile to the world.

There are several points to be made with regard to this passage.[13]

1. The passage begins with *he is dry* and continues with *she is dry*.

2. *Sons cry out*. Why does this belong here, and what does it mean? It is certainly true that when blessings do not rise on high, there is no flow of emanation to influence the lower [world],[14] but this is nothing new. What is it doing here?

3. "They cry out below in unification." Why was the unification of *Hear, O Israel* singled out, for it would seem [7b] that [such a

12. The "dryness" referred to in the passage is the cessation of the "flow" of divine emanation through the sefirot, where "river" symbolizes the sefirah Yesod and "garden" symbolizes Malkhut. Cordovero makes this connection explicit in pt. II, chap. 4, below.

13. The posing of questions concerning the passage to be discussed is characteristic of Cordovero's method of textual exposition. Earlier examples of this methodology may be found in the writings of two fifteenth-century philosophers and Biblical exegetes, Isaac Abravanel and Isaac Arama. See Marc Saperstein, *Jewish Preaching, 1200-1800: An Anthology* (New Haven: Yale University Press, 1989), p. 75.

14. The Kabbalists developed a theory that the flow of divine emanation which sustains the universe is dependent upon the Jewish people praying and performing the commandments properly. An interruption in the upward flow of blessings would thus interrupt the life-giving flow of emanation.

statement] requests neither blessing nor emanation? Let them, rather, recite a prayer consisting of blessings.

4. *Sons cry out below.* Which "sons" are these? If they are righteous, then why is there no answer? [Such an absence of response] would not be worthy of them. It would have been better to say "they" cry out below rather than "sons" [to indicate] that these are the ones who have caused the "removal" and the "dryness."

5. "This concerns one who removes." The implication is that his punishment is nothing other than *Then they will call to Me [and I will not answer]*, whereas [that punishment] does not stem from [this] but rather [from the sin of the one] "who causes [that they should not attempt to acquire them]."

6. "Who removes Kabbalah and wisdom." This is redundant.

7. "Who causes that they should not attempt." Why this lengthy repetition? If he believes this, then either it does or does not suffice. If he does not believe this, either he will assert it or not. What is the difference? This matter surely cries out for investigation.

8. "It is as if he removed." Why does the text read this way, since [the man's] intention is praiseworthy and in accordance with what appears to him to be the plain meaning of the text? Even if he is not to be praised, how is he responsible for the removal of the flow?

9. The passage enumerates four things that [this man] causes. They are *formlessness and void, poverty and length of exile.* How are they connected, and how do they emanate from him?

10. The passage does not seem to be presenting a real incident. If so, what is its purpose? Also, while we are on the subject, we may ask this question of each passage in the words of our sages where they state "It is as if the world had returned to

formlessness and void."[15] What is the purpose [of this phrase]?

Certainly the intention of [the passage] is that the letters of the word *in the beginning* (*br'syt*) should be rearranged to make the words *'rt ybs* ("dry river"). There is no doubt that the word *'rt* means "river," similar to the word *'ryt'*, which signifies "irrigation ditch,"[16] and which our sages have taken to mean a dry river. Since the verse mentions only one removal of the overflow—from the "river"[17] and not from the "pool"[18]—[the passage] states, "Here *the river dries up and is parched*." The verse indicates that since there is no flow in the "river," there is also none in the "sea."[19] Thus it is written, *The waters of the sea fail, and the river dries up and is parched*. The reason [8a] that the flow of emanation left Malkhut is because that "'*river*' *dries up and is parched*." The dryness of the "river" causes the drying up of the "sea." Thus once Scripture indicates the dryness of the "river," the dryness of the "sea" is understood as a matter of course, for the two are interconnected, since it is known that there is no water in the "sea" except from the "river."

At that time. The intention is to explain the end of the verse *[In the beginning] God created [heaven and earth]* (Gen. 1:1). The passage states, "At that time when he is dry and she is dry." This indicates that after the emanation which had been deposited with it has been expended and no [further] emanation reaches it, the "river" will also be dry and parched. Thus "he is dry and she is dry."

15. E.g., Shabbat 68a.
16. Baba Kamma 50b.
17. This is a sefirotic reference to the concept of the flow of emanation from Tiferet, through Yesod, to Malkhut.
18. This is a sefirotic reference to Malkhut, which serves as a receptacle for emanation from the rest of the sefirot and a conduit for that emanation to flow to the created universe.
19. This is a sefirotic reference to Malkhut. Cf. n. 14 above.

It is known that "river" signifies the mystery and continuity of *vav.*[20] It is also known that [in this manner] emanation is removed from [the sefirah] Tiferet,[21] which is [identified with] *vav,* though [it is] not completely [removed]. Thus [Tiferet] does not experience an absolute dryness but rather one in which there still remains some moisture, though no water. In [the sefirah] Yesod,[22] which is below [Tiferet], there may be [absolute] dryness. That is why [the passage] states *the river dries up*—from the perspective of Tiferet—*and is parched*—from the perspective of Yesod.

Possibly [the verse] *In the beginning God created* refers to the dryness of all three [sefirot],[23] with the word *God* ['Elohim] signifying Malkhut.[24] Rabbi Simeon bar Yoḥai, peace upon him, often stated this. Now the dryness of Tiferet, Yesod, and Malkhut is mentioned in the verse, with "dry river" referring to Yesod.

Alternatively it is possible that [the word *br'syt* can be rearranged] as *t'r ybs* ("dry form") as in [the verse] *Joseph was well formed* [*t'r*] *and handsome* (Gen. 39:6). *Created* [in the verse would thus] refer to Tiferet, which "created" on high.[25] And, as Rabbi Simeon bar Yoḥai explained many times, 'Elohim signifies Malkhut. Therefore heaven and earth,[26] experiencing this dryness,

20. *Vav* is the third letter of the Tetragrammaton, the four-letter Name of God (*Yod Heh Vav Heh*). It is sefirotically identified with Tiferet.

21. Tiferet emerges in Kabbalistic literature as central in the sefirotic system. Its union with Malkhut is crucial to the sustained emanation of divine energy to create and maintain the universe.

22. Yesod's position in Kabbalistic literature is essentially that of a conduit for emanation between Tiferet and Malkhut.

23. I.e., Tiferet, Yesod, Malkhut.

24. Each divine name is connected by Kabbalists with an individual sefirah. In this case, 'Elohim refers to the sefirah Malkhut. Cf. pt. VII, below.

25. From the union of Tiferet and Malkhut, all souls are created. Cf. Matt, *Zohar,* p. 217.

26. Tiferet and Malkhut.

together cry out the unification [of the Shema] and *there is no voice in response*, as we will explain with God's help. Thus [returning to the verse] *and the earth*, which refers to *the river and the sea will be dry and parched*, *was formless and void*, as we will explain.

Alternatively, *God* ['Elohim] *created* signifies the righteous, for they are the sons which *God created*, the sons of the Shekhinah.[27] These holy souls cry out below. *Heaven and earth* refers to the unification [of the Shema Yisrael]—and is there no one listening? God forbid! In this way it is easy [to comprehend] the phrase "sons cry out below."

If [8b] [you were to say] that all this is no problem, seeing that one sinner can destroy much good, nonetheless [the passage] carefully stated *Hear, O Israel*, referring to Tiferet and Malkhut. *Heaven and earth* indicates an actual unification. Thus the passage would mean that even if they came to perform a unification,[28] [an action] which seemingly rectifies the [sefirotic] separation, this [rectification] is nonetheless impossible to accomplish, particularly through prayer. This is why *heaven and earth* was specifically mentioned, for it signifies unification. Despite this there is *no voice*, referring to the Holy One, blessed be He,[29] and *no answer*, referring to His Shekhinah.[30] This is why [Scripture] states, *The earth was*

27. Shekhinah is the term for the (female) Divine Presence. It is identified by Kabbalists with the sefirah Malkhut. For the significance of the term "sons of God," see n. 23 above.

28. The purpose of prayer for the Kabbalists is to achieve the unification of Tiferet and Malkhut so as to ensure an unimpeded flow of divine emanation. To this day, many Jews preface the recitation of blessings with the phrase *le-shem yiḥud kudsha brikh hu u-shekhintei* "[I do this] for the sake of the unification of the Holy One, blessed be He, and His Shekhinah." In an early Kabbalistic text, the spiritual intention of the Shema prayer specifically refers to the unification of the ten sefirot. See Idel, *Kabbalah*, p. 55. Cf. nn. 12 and 19 above.

29. Tiferet.

30. Malkhut.

formless and void. The earth—the Holy One, blessed be He, and His Shekhinah—*was formless and void,* or, in other words, *dry and parched.* Since it might seem farfetched to say that they would not succeed if they come to effect a reparation and unification, he proved the matter from the verse, *Then they will call upon Me [and I will not answer].* This indicates that they actually recited *Hear, O Israel,* calling upon them, [Tiferet and Malkhut, to unify,] and [the result was that] *I will not answer*—God forbid.

The verse is not [ostensibly] written concerning this. Moreover, it is possible to say that [this interpretation of] the verse presents a difficulty; for why would God *not answer* after the rectification of the separation? Therefore the verse [must be] interpreted [to mean] that their sin affects the upper spheres and thus they have no means to rectify it.[31] This is why [the passage] states "This concerns one who removes [Kabbalah and wisdom]," which relates to the verse *Then they will call upon Me [and I will not answer].*

The preceding verse states, *Wisdom [cries out] in the streets* (Prov. 1:20). This verse refers to the recondite secrets of our holy Torah. [Wisdom] states, *How long will you simple ones love simplicity?* (Prov. 1:22). In other words, you who follow after the simple meaning[32] deceive yourselves with your love of simplicity—the part of the Torah you do believe in—which contains nothing beyond the simple meaning. *And scoffers [be eager] to scoff.* This has reference to [King] Manasseh [son of Hezekiah], who would expound [difficult *haggadot* and say, "Did Moses have only to write *The sister of Lotan was Timna* (Gen. 36:22)]?"[33]

31. The upper three sefirot, Keter, Ḥokhmah, and Binah, are considered by Kabbalists to be relatively inaccessible to human intellects. Hence human beings would not able to affect their separation in the same way that they can affect the "lower" sefirot.

32. *Peshat.* This refers to the simple, literal meaning of a given text.

33. Sanhedrin 99b.

Who has caused these people to chase after the simple meaning [of Scripture] and ignore the esoteric portions? It is *you dullards [who] hate knowledge* (Prov. 1:23), meaning the knowledge of hidden things. What is written [in the verse] after that? *You are indifferent to my rebuke, I will now speak my mind to you.* This means that the soul which is enwrapped in the simple meaning [is now addressed]: *I will now speak my mind to you and let* [9a] *you know my thoughts* concerning the secrets which I possess. *And you spurned [my counsel]* (Prov. 1:25) . . . *Then they will call upon me [but I will not answer* (Prov. 1:28). This is why [the passage] states, "This concerns one who removes Kabbalah and wisdom. [Kabbalah] means the written Torah, [which symbolizes] Tiferet, and [wisdom] refers to the oral Torah, which is Malkhut. This is the mystery of the *vav heh* in which the *yod heh* is concealed,[34] as it is written, *The hidden things are for the Lord our God.* There the secret of God is revealed—*to us and our children forever* (Deut. 29:28).

Thus one who denies the mysteries of the Torah and its esoteric lore causes the "removal of wisdom," *yod*, "and Kabbalah," *heh*, from Tiferet and Malkhut, *vav* and *heh*, referring to the written and oral Torah.[35] Since it is difficult for one [to understand] how the poor man, who can only believe what his eyes see, could sin [so grievously] as to be punished by having the *yod heh* removed from the *vav heh* [in the divine Name], [the passage] states that we are dealing only with one who teaches this publicly and acts according to his teaching. This is the reason that [the passage] states "[He] who causes that they should not attempt [to acquire] them and who

34. Cf. n. 18 above.

35. In sefirotic symbolism "Wisdom" refers to the sefirah Ḥokhmah, and "Kabbalah" to the sefirah Binah. Ḥokhmah and Binah are considered by Kabbalists to be in union in the same manner as Tiferet and Malkhut among the "lower" sefirot. The written Torah symbolizes Tiferet, while the oral Torah is Malkhut.

asserts that there is nothing beyond the plain meaning of the Torah"—the written Torah—"and Talmud"—the oral Torah. The man who has done this has caused a "dryness" above as surely as if he had sinned with his very hands. This is why [the passage] states, "It is as if he removed the flow from that river," i.e., *vav*,[36] "and that garden," i.e., *heh*,[37] which constitute the written and oral Torahs.

"Woe to him. It were better for him had he never been created," since he has caused harm on high, "and had never taught," for through his "study" of the written and oral Torah he takes Tiferet and Malkhut and removes from them the mystery of *yod* and *heh*. Thus in his very Torah study he causes loss and division, so that the study becomes a sin. It is doubtless concerning him that [the verse] states, *And to the wicked God says* (Ps. 50:16), for it is considered as if he [had returned the world to *formlessness and void*]. In truth there exists *formlessness and void* [on the side of] good and *formlessness and void* of the *kelipah*.[38] "Formlessness" (*tohu*) signifies [the sefirah] Ḥokhmah, which is a place of astonishment (*toheh*). "Void" (*bohu*) is that which clothes the formlessness. It signifies [the sefirah] Binah.[39] By means of these [two sefirot] the *formlessness and void* of the *kelipah* are nullified. [9b] Thus everyone who removes these two [sefirotic] qualities and causes the "outer ones" to prevail can surely [be considered] as if [he had caused] the world to return to *formlessness and void*. He removes the world which is the dwelling place of the *formlessness and void*[40] of the Holy One, blessed be He, and causes the "outer

36. Tiferet.
37. Malkhut.
38. *Kelipah* is the Kabbalistic term for the forces of evil, which are organized in a "counter-sefirotic" system of their own.
39. Binah is the "mother" of the seven "lower" sefirot.
40. I.e., Ḥokhmah and Binah.

ones"[41] to rule. Thus the world is clothed in the *kelipah*, which constitutes the primordial *formlessness and void.* This is why [Scripture] states, *And the earth was formless and void,* for there was no emanation from the supernal *formlessness and void,* as I have explained.

This defect, therefore, is the mystery of *yod heh,*[42] which refers to wisdom and Kabbalah.[43] This he removes, causing "poverty" in place of the "riches" emanating from Tiferet, which is the mystery of the river mentioned previously. "Length of exile" is the mystery of the "waters" left the "sea" [signifying that] the Shekhinah left for exile.[44] This was explained by Rabbi Simeon bar Yoḥai, peace upon him, in another place. [He stated] that the mystery of *the earth was formless and void* [refers to the period] after the destruction of the First and Second Temples. *And God said, "Let there be light"* (Gen. 1:3)—this [refers] to the mystery of the future redemption. I dealt with this matter in my book, *Or Yakar.*[45]

With this the passage has been explained and we have uncovered the sin of those who hold this opinion. First of all, [the sin] involves the removal of emanation and [the separation of] Ḥokhmah and Binah from Tiferet and Malkhut. Secondly, it is as if the world had returned to *formlessness and void.* Thirdly, it causes "poverty". Fourthly, [it causes] "length of exile," as I have explained.

41. I.e., the *kelipah.*

42. The first two letters of the Tetragrammaton. Cf. n. 18 above.

43. Ḥokhmah and Binah. Cf. n. 33 above.

44. See n. 23 above.

45. Moses Cordovero, *Or Yakar,* vol. 1 (Jerusalem, 1965), pt. I, sec. 1. The relevant passage is Zohar I, 25b.

2

More on This Matter

In [the Zohar], section Be-ha'alotekha [III, 152a], it states:
Rabbi Simeon said;
Woe to that son of man who says that this Torah has come to present an ordinary story and ordinary words. For if this were so, even in this time we would be able to make a Torah of ordinary words; [one] better than any of them.
If [the Torah] comes merely to present ordinary words, then there are even greater words among the nobles of the world.
If so, let us seek [those words] and make a Torah of them.
However, all the words of the Torah are [sublime].
Come and see:
The upper world and the lower world are evenly balanced: Israel below and the high angels [10a] above. Of the lofty angels it is written, *He makes His angels as winds* (Ps. 104:4).
This [refers to their state] in the high place.
When they come down to earth [the angels] clothe themselves in the garments of this world.
Had they not clothed themselves in garments after the fashion of this world, they would not have been able to exist in this world, and the world would not suffer them [to exist].
If this is so with regard to the angels, then [how much more so] with regard to the Torah, which created them and all the worlds, and everything exists for its sake.[1]

1. The Torah as the raison d'être for the creation of the universe is a common Midrashic theme. See, for example, Bereshit Rabbah 1:4.

When [the Torah] did come down into the world, were it not clothed in the garments of this world, the world would not have been able to suffer it.
Therefore the story of the Torah constitutes its garment.
He who thinks that the garment is actually the Torah and and not something else, let his spirit deflate and let him have no portion in the world-to-come.
It was in this connection that David said, *Open my eye that I may behold wondrous things out of your Torah* (Ps. 119:18), [meaning] that which is under the garment is really Torah.
Come and see:
A garment is visible to all.
Those fools, when they see a man in a garment that appears good to them, seek no farther.
They think that the garment is the actual thing.
[However,] the essence of the body is the soul.
Just so, the Torah has a body.
The commandments of the Torah are called the "body" of the Torah.[2]
This body is clothed in a garment made up of the stories of this world.
The fools of the world look on nothing save the garment, which is the story of the Torah [and nothing more. They do not look at that which is under the garment].[3]
The wise, who worship the Most High King, those who stood at Mount Sinai,[4] look only at the soul,[5] which is the most essential thing of all.

2. Cf. Mishnah, Ḥagigah 1:8.

3. The sentence in brackets was omitted by Cordovero, who indicated the omission with the word "etc."

4. According to rabbinic tradition, *all* Jews, whether alive at the time or not, participated in the revelation at Sinai. See Shemot Rabbah 28:6. The Zohar III, 179b, states: "One who strives to study Torah—it is as if he stood all the day on Mount Sinai and received the Torah." The implication of the Zohar's statement is that no one is truly worthy to be called a Jew unless he knows Kabbalah.

5. This refers to Kabbalah.

It is the true Torah.
In the world-to-come, they will look at the soul of the soul of the Torah.
Come and see.
Thus it is above:
There is garment and body and soul and soul of souls.
The heavens and their host are the garment.
The congregation of Israel[6] is the body which receives the soul, [10b] which is the glory [Tiferet] of Israel, which is the very Torah.
The soul of the soul is the ancient Holy One.[8]
All are connected one to the other.
Woe to those sinners of the world who say that this Torah is nothing but an ordinary story.
They look at the garment and no farther.
Happy are the righteous who regard the Torah properly.
Wine cannot stay except in a jar.
So Torah cannot abide except in this garment.
Because of this one must seek to look at [the Torah] only only through what exists under the garment.
Thus all those words and stories are garments.

In this passage, [the Zohar] has instructed us concerning the refutation of the opinion of this group and those like them who denigrate the esoteric portion of our holy Torah. Essentially, we learn from [the passage] that over and above the secret inherent in the matter there is an even more hidden level of mystery which is presently unknown even to those who know [Kabbalah]. Nonetheless we and all Israel will be privileged [to behold] this [mystery] in the future world.

6. An appellation of Malkhut.
7. A reference to the sefirah Tiferet.
8. A reference to the highest and most mysterious of the sefirot, Keter.

Now, brethren, explain to me how a person who has never beheld the soul [of the Torah in this world] will, in the future, gaze upon the soul of the soul? Such a person will be found wanting in the future [world]. Do not reply that some are unworthy [to behold] her, for there is a great difference between one who denies her and one who does not deny her and yet has never beheld [her] light. Superior to both of them is the one who has pursued her.

The Lord, the living God and eternal King, sits in judgment to clear the innocent and declare the culprit guilty. *He apportions to man according to his ways* (Jer. 17:10). The words of our sages, their memory be a blessing, cannot be denied. [They stated] in Midrash Mishlei:[9] "They ask a man [on the Day of Judgment], 'Have you gazed upon the *Merkavah*?[10] Have you beheld my *Shi'ur Koma*?"[11] Copying this [entire] passage would be too cumbersome. Rabbi Simeon bar Yoḥai, peace upon him, also dealt with this matter in the Zohar, same section, page 149.[12] Read it there.

9. *Midrash Shoḥer Tov 'al Mishlei* (Jerusalem, 1968), p. 16. The relevant section of the midrash reads as follows: "One comes [to divine judgment] who has studied Talmud. The Holy One, blessed be He, says to him: My son, since you have occupied yourself in Talmud, have you gazed upon the *Merkavah*? Have you looked . . . upon My Throne of Glory? . . . What is the measurement of My palm? What is the measurement of the toes of My feet?" For Cordovero, the importance of this particular midrash is that it implies that Talmudic learning is not in itself sufficient. Cf. Burton Visotsky, *Midrash Mishle* (New York, 1990), p. 84.

10. The divine vehicle described in Ezekiel 1. In rabbinic literature, the term came to refer to esoteric doctrine. See Mishnah, Ḥagigah 3:1.

11. Literally "Measurement of the Body." It refers to the fantastic measurements ascribed to the body of the divine "Glory" (*kavod*) in the literature of early Jewish mysticism. See Scholem, *Kabbalah*, pp. 16-18; M. S. Cohen, *The Shiur Qomah* (Lanham, Md.: University Press of America, 1983); P. Schaefer, *Synopse zur Hekhalot Literatur* (Tuebingen, 1981); Yosef Dan, *Ha-Mistikah ha-'Ivrit ha-Kedumah* (Tel-Aviv: Misrad ha-Bittaḥon, 1989).

12. Zohar III, 149: "He who says that this story of the Torah comes to indicate [the significance] of that story alone, let his spirit deflate! For if this were so, it would not be the lofty Torah, the Torah of truth."

[11a]

3

There is a second group which avoids this science with various arguments, though all [its members] admit the eminence of the discipline. Some say that not all are worthy to enter into the study of [such] sublime wisdom. They even imagine, in their zealousness for the Lord of Hosts and His Torah, that they must punish those who pursue it, since they feel that [the Kabbalists] have dared to deal with matters divine, beyond the ken of most people. These matters[, they say,] must not be dealt with by men of little worth. When one presses them [regarding] the ancients who pursued [this subject], they reply: "Who are we [in comparison] with them, *the holy ones on the earth* (Ps. 16:3), [that we should deal] with these lofty mysteries?"[1]

[Then] there are those who assert that delving into this science is truly worthwhile. However, [they further state that] this subject requires a qualified teacher, and in their opinion, no [teacher] exists who has penetrated to the very depths of [the discipline].[2] They have, therefore, avoided listening to even elementary propositions. When they hear those engaged [in Kabbalah] speak of it, whether

1. It is a commonplace in rabbinic Judaism to assume that previous generations were inherently more knowledgeable in Torah. Cf. Shabbat 112b: "If the first [sages] were as angels, then we are as men; if they were as men, then we are as donkeys."

2. An exemplar of this attitude is R. Levi ibn Ḥabib (ca. 1483-1545), an elder contemporary of Cordovero who lived in both Safed and Jerusalem. In his responsa (Venice, 1565, no. 8), he stated that he had not succeeded in studying Kabbalah "since man was not given permission to understand it by himself and investigate it. Rather, as its name implies, he needs to receive it from a master who also received it. In this era and in our countries men who are perfect in it are not to be found."

little or much, they open their mouths and smoothly say: "May God forgive you, for your sin is great and you do not understand what you are doing. Would that we were able to understand this subject, which is beyond you. [However,] when all is said and done, no one understands this science, and [hence] you and we are equal [in our understanding] of this matter." These poor people believe that there is no difference between one who serves God and one who serves Him not.

There are also those who imagine that before pursuing [Kabbalah], they must first master the science of astronomy.[3] They have other notions which keep them from [following] the straight path. They sanctimoniously give themselves the excuse that their bellies are not yet full of the bread and meat of the Gemara.[4] For these poor people, their entire lives will not be sufficient to learn even a bit of [Gemara], let alone to fill their bellies so that they could partake of this science and be sated. Thus the poor people go to their eternal rest bereft of wisdom. There are a number of other cases which fall under these two categories [11b] which we have dealt with.

Concerning people of these three types, we may say that, although their intention is to exalt this science, they are, truthfully, not qualified to speak of it. Who should come and testify—one who has not observed the moon or one who has?[5] True it is that

3. Maimonides, in *Guide of the Perplexed* 1.34, states that prior to commencing the study of the "divine science," one must first have trained in logic, mathematics, and the natural sciences. In his "Epistle Dedicatory" to the *Guide*, Maimonides spoke specifically of astronomy as one of the sciences preparing the reader to understand the secrets of the Torah. Cf. Harry A. Wolfson, *Studies in the History of Philosophy and Religion*, vol. 1 (Cambridge, Mass., 1973), pp. 516-517.

4. Cf. Maimonides, *Mishneh Torah*, Hilkhot Yesodei ha-Torah 4:13.

5. Witnesses to the sighting of a new moon were rigorously interrogated. See Mishnah, Rosh ha-Shanah 2:6.

this science is sublime and exalted, as we will yet indicate with God's help. However, concerning these people and their ilk, we must say [that they are] *those who speak of you with deliberate evil* (Ps. 139:20). Of them it is said, *Wisdom is too high for a fool; he dare not open his mouth in the gates* (Prov. 24:7). It is also written, *The conceited man seeks wisdom yet finds none; to one of understanding, knowledge comes easily* (Prov. 14:6). It is also written, *I love those who love me; those who search for me find me* (Prov. 8:17). There are many similar [verses] in the admonitions of King Solomon, peace upon him.

Similarly, King David, peace upon him, stated, *You, God, are my portion, I have promised to keep Your word* (Ps. 119:57). This means that, in order to keep the word of God, I may not abase myself. Concerning this it is said, *Do not be overly righteous* (Eccles. 7:16). I, however, declare that God is my portion. My soul has a portion in God on high, and I am as worthy of the word of God as one of the ministering angels.

4

There is a third group which shuns this science on the grounds that man is liable to err in such matters and possibly come to sin, falling into one of the errors which appertain to this lofty area. The intentions of this group are certainly good. However their actions are not acceptable.[1] They are indeed correct when they say that man is liable to err in these recondite matters. Nonetheless, [even if one does err] he will not incur sin. This was explained by our sages, their memory be a blessing, in the Book *Bahir*.[2]

> Rabbi Reḥumai's students asked him:
> "Why is it written, *a prayer of the prophet Habakkuk [upon shigeonot]* (Hab. 3:1)?
> It should rather state, *a psalm.*"
> Now everyone who removes himself from the affairs of the world and occupies himself with the Account of the Chariot[3] is accepted before the Holy One, blessed be He, as though he had prayed all day.
> Thus it is said, *a prayer.*
> What is *shigeonot?*
> It is as You [God] said:
> *With her love you will continually be infatuated* (Prov. 5:19).
> What is the meaning of this?
> [It refers to] the Account of the Chariot.

1. Cf. Judah ha-Levi, *Kuzari* 1.1. Ha-Levi begins his work with a description of a dream of the king of the Khazars in which an angel informs him that his way of thinking is indeed pleasing to the Creator but not his way of acting.

2. *Bahir*, chap. 68.

3. See above, chap. 2, n. 10.

Now there are [some] points to be raised:

1. "Why [is it written] [12a] *a prayer* . . . It should rather state *a psalm.*" Why should "psalm" (*tehillah*) be preferable to "prayer" (*tefillah*)? If it is because the verses do not contain any prayer at all, why must we have "psalm" rather than "song" (*mizmor*) or "poem" (*shir*) or (*mikhtam*), or similar words?[4] Moreover, [even] if there is no "prayer" in these verses, there is likewise no [psalm of] praise or glorification. Truly neither "prayer" nor "psalm" ought to be [written].

2. "Now everyone who removes himself." Who told him this? Does the difference in the wording between "psalm" and "prayer" indicate that he was removing himself from anything?

3. "And occupies himself with the Account of the Chariot." Who told him this? Is it because of [the word] *shigeonot*? Then what of the rest of the words of the Torah, concerning which one could also err?

4. "What is *shigeonot*?" Essentially [we must ask] what his motive was in presenting [this question] now.

5. When [the passage] states, "*With her love you will continually be infatuated.* What is the meaning of this?" Is there any proof that the verse *with her love* refers to the Account of the Chariot?

We [would have liked to] say that the meaning of the verse *a prayer of Habakkuk the prophet upon shigeonot* is that [the prophet] was praying before his Master concerning his "infatuation." This, however, is impossible for several reasons: 1. The verse does not concern itself with confession of sin, for "confession of sin" is nowhere written. [2.] Moreover [the verse] should [then] read "errors" (*shegiot* and not *shigeonot*). [Such] a verse exists: *Who can*

4. According to rabbinic literature there are ten such words. Cf. Pesaḥim 117a, Rashi on Ps. 1:1.

understand errors? (Ps. 19:13). Alternatively, [let the verse read] "mistakes' (*shegagot*).

What, then, is *shigeonot*? It is certainly derived from the word [*shigeon* as in] *shigeon of David* (Ps. 7:1), which indicates praise and glorification.[5] Thus *a prayer of Habakkuk* must [be considered] greater than all the psalms and *shigeonim* which are sung before Him. If this is so, then [the verse] would have to state "psalm," for "prayer" has no reference to [God's] praise. "[Psalms of] Praise" [are directed] above to the ten sefirot, while "prayer" [is directed] at Malkhut.[6] Thus [the verse] should state "psalm," which is a song greater than all songs, which inheres in [the sefirah] Binah, which is superior to the other praises.[7]

For this reason, [Rabbi Reḥumai] explained, "Now everyone who removes himself . . ." The intention is not that he removes himself from the concerns of this illusory world, for it is clear that there is a greater reward for one who serves God than [for] one who does not serve Him. [12b] One who is occupied with the [Account of the] Chariot is serving God; one who is occupied with affairs of this world has not served Him.[8]

The intention is rather [to indicate] that Habakkuk the prophet is "one who removes himself from the affairs of the world." Those [of his] prophecies which dealt with the affairs of the world were written prior to this prophecy. [Thus] the matter of the righteous to whom evil befalls and the wicked to whom good befalls was

5. Cf. Abraham Ibn Ezra, commentary on Ps. 7:1.

6. For Kabbalists, prayer was to be directed at specific sefirot in order to be most effective. Among his other writings, Cordovero wrote Kabbalistic commentaries on the liturgy of Rosh ha-Shanah and Yom Kippur.

7. Binah's position among the three uppermost sefirot is similar in many respects to that of Malkhut in the sefirotic system as a whole.

8. Cf. Maimonides, *Guide of the Perplexed* 3.51. There Maimonides justifies the system of commandments as a whole by stating that they train a person to occupy himself with God rather than with things of this world.

9. Cf. Hab. 1:4.

difficult for him.[9] Thus also [he dealt with] the mores of this world, which are the portions of the Torah that deal with worldly concerns.[10] After all this, the prophet left these concerns and spoke of matters concerning [the Account of] the Chariot. [Thus he] said, *God is coming from Teman . . . it is a brilliant light* (Hab. 3:3-4).

Therefore *a prayer of Habakkuk the prophet* refers to an important prayer of Habakkuk when he abandoned those portions of the Torah [dealing] with matters of this world and occupied himself with the [Account of the] Chariot. This is the reason that [the passage] states: "What is *shigeonot*?"

Thus if we were to say that "prayer" retains its [plain] meaning, it would be possible to explain that "prayer" concerns the *shigeonot* and the "praises." Alternatively, it is possible that [Habakkuk] was praying concerning his errors, and though this might be difficult for us [to believe], since there is no confession [of sin in the passage], I might believe that the verse is being elliptic.

However, now that he has explicated *a prayer*, as we have explained concerning the meaning of *shigeonot*, his answer is that it is the same case as in the verse, *With her love you will continually be infatuated.* If this refers to a portion of the Torah which necessarily [leads to] error, I would say that it must be the [Account of the] Chariot, so that one might say *With her love you will continually err*,[11] meaning that because of love of the Torah you will err.

[But] this is astonishing! How does one err in loving [Torah]? On the contrary, he who desires Torah should never come to error. Because of his desire, he will occupy himself with it and will not

10. Hab. 2:4 ff.

11. This reinterpretation of Prov. 5:19 understands the word *tishgeh* in the sense of "error" and not "infatuation."

err. However, this certainly refers to the Account of the Chariot, which [is something] man desires. Because of the greatness of his desire, he peers into esoteric matters, and it is impossible for him not to fail [in his understanding]. Nonetheless, this [failure] is [forgiven him] charitably [and] accounted for him "as though he had prayed all the day." The reason that a man will not be caught [in sin] if he should err in a matter of this nature will be made clear, with God's help.

Do not [attempt] to refute me [with the case of] Elisha [ben Avuya].[12] There are several reasons why [this case is] not [relevant]. First of all, there we are dealing with heresy, God forbid. [13a] *It is a fire which consumes down to Abaddon* (Job 31:12). Secondly, he has already explained [that it has to be other] than Elisha "the Other One" in that [in this case the one who "errs"] recognizes his master . . .

My way of explaining this passage is different. Some of it I have dealt with in the commentary on *Ra'ya Mehemna*, where it is taught that "psalm" (*tehillah*) refers to Malkhut.[13] In the *Tikkunim* it states that "prayer" refers to Malkhut with reference to the ten types of praise of which the Book of Psalms is composed.[14] There is no contradiction [here] since "psalm" and "prayer" refer to Malkhut in its two aspects. When one prays out of distress and need, then [Malkhut] is called "prayer," since [in this instance] she bears the prayers of Israel on high. That is the essence of "prayer," as is

12. Elisha ben Avuya was a rabbinic sage and the teacher of R. Meir. According to several rabbinic sources, he became a heretic and was referred to as *Aḥer*, "the Other One." In Tosefta, Ḥagigah 2:3, his heresy is traced to the fact that he was one of four rabbis who entered *Pardes* (understood as the study of esoteric lore), out of which only R. Akiva emerged unscathed.

13. Zohar III, 227b. Cf. also III, 101a.

14. *Tikkunei Zohar*, 2b. Cf. Zohar I, 23b. Cf. also n. 4 above.

explained in that place and elsewhere. When a miracle is wrought for a man and he feels a need to say words of praise, then [Malkhut] is a "psalm" in the mystery of the miracle, which stems from Yesod [and] which brings her to union with Tiferet, which is called "praise" (*hallel*). Hence she is called "psalm" (*tehillah*), from the word "light," as it is written, *When his lamp shone* (*be-hillo*) *upon my head* (Job 29:3). For she brings life to man through the miracle which is Yesod [stemming from] the "Tree of Life," which is Tiferet, which [in turn] derives life from Binah, which is [also] called "psalm." [Binah] is also [called] the *land of the living* (Ps. 142:6). Life [comes] from [Binah] through the force of Ḥokhmah, as it is written, *Wisdom* (*ḥokhmah*) *will give life to him who possesses it* (Eccles. 7:12).

Now [the passage] states that, according to the prophet, "prayer" should not suffice, for Malkhut is not [manifested] to him [in its mode of] "prayer." However, [psalm of] "praise" would suffice, for he is praising the mystery of life which has influenced him. For Habakkuk was the son of the Shunamite woman to whom life was given from on high.[15]

Thus [the passage] states: "It should rather state, *a psalm*," as [Habakkuk] said, *O Lord, [I am awed by] Your works. Renew them in these years* (Hab. 3:2). For this reason, [the passage] explained, "Now everyone who removes himself from the affairs of the world . . ."

The significance of this [passage] is that there are two ways to approach prayer. The first [way] is that of "slaves who serve their master in order to receive a reward" (Avot 1:3). Thus their prayer [is meant] according to the literal meaning with regard to their enjoyment [of the pleasures] of this world. To such [worshippers], prayer

15. Cf. Zohar I, 7b; II, 44b-45a.

[consists] of asking God for their sustenance in the lower [world]. However, there are children [of God] whose entire purpose in prayer is to unify Malkhut with Tiferet. This is the mystery [13b] of "psalm" which he interpreted as partaking of the mystery of "praise" (*hallel*). Thus, through their prayer they abandon the matters of this world and occupy themselves with the Account of the Chariot, which is the mystery [of the divine name] *Y'HDOVNHY.*[16] For the union of the Holy One, blessed be He, and His Shekhinah is termed the Account of the Chariot, which is [equivalent to] "psalm."

[However,] lest one think that since [the worshipper] does not pursue his [mundane] needs he does not receive a reward and benefit from this world, God forbid, the verse considers him "as though he had prayed all the day." This is [the meaning of the verse] *Cast your burden upon the Lord and He will sustain you* (Ps. 55:23). Thus the man's intent is the unification [of Tiferet and Malkhut] and the needs of his [eternal] world. He seeks nothing save that [God] should sustain him. Thus [his utterance] was called "prayer." Though he was occupied with the mystery of the unification and [related] matters, [nonetheless] he is aided with regard to the affairs of the world "as though he had prayed all the day." Now when [the passage] states: "What is *shigeonot?*", [implying] that it should have been called [something] different, we now understand that ["prayer"] ranks above "psalm" and is more honorable than *shigeonot* and praises (*shebaḥim*). Thus he explained [that *shigeonot* is] a word connoting error . . .

This is also found in the Book *Bahir.*[17]

16. This is a combination of the two divine names, YHVH and ADoNaY. On the Kabbalistic use of divine names, see Moshe Idel, *Kabbalah: New Perspectives* (New Haven, 1988), pp. 96-123. Concerning this particular divine name, see Mark Verman, "The Development of *Yihudim* in Spanish Kabbalah," *Jerusalem Studies in Jewish Thought* 8 (1989): 25-42.

17. *Bahir,* chap. 150. Cf. Gittin 43a.

Rabbi Reḥumai said:
"Why is it written, *The way to life is the rebuke that disciplines* (Prov. 6:23)?
This teaches that everyone who is familiar with the Account of the Chariot and the Account of Creation cannot but fail.
Thus it is written, *Let this ruin be under your care* (Isa. 3:6).
These are matters in which no man can succeed unless he fails in them.
The Torah speaks of the *rebuke that disciplines.* But truly [through it] he merits *the way to life.*"

There are points to be made:

1. "This teaches that everyone who is familiar." How can the verse demonstrate this?

2. "[He] cannot but fail." Why is it impossible [for him] not to fail? It is perhaps possible that he should fail [given the subject of his inquiry]. However, why should it state "[He] cannot but fail"? Is [the passage] not sufficient without this?

3. *Let this ruin.* What is the meaning of this verse here?

4. "The Torah speaks of *the rebuke that disciplines.*" What is being said and what does it mean?

5. "But truly [through it] he merits." How do we derive this from the verse?

Moreover [14a] there is a confusion in his statements [so that they appear] out of order. Thus we might say that he had intended [to deal] with the beginning of the verse, *For the commandment is a lamp.* Our sages, their memory be a blessing, explained, "Sin extinguishes a commandment, *but the Torah is a light,* for it is so great that no sin can extinguish Torah" (Sotah 21b). Thus, according to this [passage], how can one who possesses Torah in sin make expiation? [Through] *the way to life*—he will merit eternal life.

But how is the sin to be requited? [Through] *the rebuke that disciplines*, [meaning] through suffering. This is the explanation of the verse. However, there is a difficulty with this [interpretation]. [According to it,] if a man should sin and continually commit iniquity and [even] possess in his hands a majority of sins, he would [still] merit [eternal] life. This is very farfetched! On the contrary, it was written concerning this *But to the wicked God says, "Who are you to recite My laws?"* (Ps. 50:16).

Rather the intention [of the passage] is that this "sin" is not an actual sin, as one might have thought. On the contrary, it teaches that "one who is familiar with the Account of Creation and the Account of the Chariot cannot but fail." The reason [for this] is that when a man is occupied with the remainder of the laws of the Torah, his mind will consider points of contradiction at the beginning of [his] analysis. He may declare the impure [to be] pure, and similar [things]. However, "dryness"[18] does not result from this at all. On the contrary, he will continue his analysis until he comes to the truth [regarding] the law. Alternatively, his colleagues will make him come [to realize his error]. In this [process], he has not sinned at all. This is not the case [regarding] the Account of the Chariot and the Account of Creation, for if he is mistaken in one of the esoteric matters, he has thereby believed in something that is not proper.

[Moreover,] these are matters which depend on pure faith. Therefore it is impossible to evaluate their contradictions and not err in one point [or another]. Concerning such a sin it was said, *sin does not extinguish Torah*. On the contrary, he will in the end acknowledge the truth. Whatever harm ensued from his [erroneous] thought will be purified through "rebuke" in this world, and he will be [considered] innocent in the world-to-come.

18. This "dryness" refers to the state in which, because of sin, the flow of divine energy through the sefirotic system is interrupted. See above, chap. 1, n. 10.

[The passage] made this explanation necessary when it stated, *Let this ruin be under your care.* This [passage] was written after the verse: *For behold, the Lord, the Lord of Hosts, will remove from Jerusalem and from Judah prop and stay* (Isa. 3:6). [14b] This is a metaphor for the wisdoms and the wise. It is [further] written: *For a man shall take hold of his brother of the house of his father: "You have a mantle; [be our ruler]"* (Isa. 3:6). That is [to say], you have mastered subjects which are covered with a mantle, such as the Account of the Chariot and the Account of Creation. Therefore it is proper that you be our leader and guide us in them. *Let this ruin* means that which will ensue from this failure and sin. *Be under your care* means that he will undergo suffering because of this.

He will respond: *In that day he will swear: "I will not be a healer"* (Isa. 3:7), since I do not have the knowledge either in revealed or in esoteric [wisdom]. Thus it is [further] written: *In my hand there is neither bread nor a mantle; you shall not make me [a ruler].*

From this [passage] one can see that there are necessarily subjects in which no man can succeed unless he fails in them. [When] the Torah speaks of *the rebuke that disciplines*, it does not mean, God forbid, that God abandons that person or thrusts him down. On the contrary, the *rebuke that disciplines* tries him with "rebuke" in this world because of his sins.

[Now] following this [line of reasoning] you [might] say that it would be worthwhile for a man to distance himself from a science through which he will bring "rebuke" upon himself. [However, in refutation to] this it states that, on the contrary, such a person truly merits *the path of life.*

Accordingly, the verse means that *the path of life* consists of *the rebuke that disciplines* which a man suffers according to his sins. He will [then] be cleansed to merit *the path of life*, as if he had never erred in his life.

5

Besides the material which was expounded in the previous chapter, there is a marvelous passage in the Zohar, section Kedoshim [III, 85a]:

Do not place a stumbling block before the blind (Lev. 19:14).
This refers to one who has not yet acquired [the competence] to teach and yet instructs.
Thus they taught:
It is written, *For she has cast down many wounded; a mighty host are all her slain* (Prov. 7:26).
This person transgressed because of *Do not place a stumbling block before the blind.*
Thus he caused his companions to be found wanting in the world-to-come.
We have learned:
He who walks the straight path in Torah [study] and he who attempts [to master] the Torah properly has a portion in the world-to-come.
For the word [of Torah] which goes out of his mouth [15a] traverses the world and mounts on high.
How many lofty holy beings join in that word which goes on the straight path and is crowned with a holy crown.
It swims in the river of the world-to-come which goes forth from Eden.
[The word] is received by it and absorbed in its midst.
The lofty tree is planted round about that river.
Thus comes forth the supernal light which crowns that man all the day, just as we learned.
[However, with regard to] the one who labors in the Torah and does not know how to master her in the straight path—[His]

word goes and roams on paths with no one to join it.
All thrust it outside, and it roams the world and does not find a place where it, which has strayed from the straight path, could be acquired.
Thus it is written, *Do not place a stumbling block before the blind.*
On account of this [it is written]: *You will fear your God; I am the Lord* (Lev. 19:14).
He who desires to labor in the Torah but finds no one to teach him:
[Yet] he labors for the love of Torah and stammers its [words] since he does not know [them].
Each and every word goes forth.
And the Holy One, blessed be He, rejoices in that word and receives it [and plants it] around that river.
Of these words are made many trees, which are called *willows of the brook* (Lev. 23:40).
Thus it is written, *In its love you will continually be infatuated.*
King David also said:
O Lord, show me the way of Your statutes (Ps. 119:33).
Worthy are those who know the paths of the Torah and strive to master it on the straight path.
For they plant trees of life greater than all remedies.
Therefore it is written, *The Torah of truth was in his mouth* (Mal. 2:6).
Is there, then, a Torah which is not true?
Yes.
It is as they say:
That one who does not know taught [something] that is not true, and taught a word that is not truth.
Because of this it was written: *The Torah of truth was in his mouth.*
Despite this [possibility] one should learn words of Torah from all men, even from one who does not know, since he will on this account awaken in [his study of the] Torah and go to learn

> from someone who does know.
> Later on [15b] it will be forgotten that he came to the Torah in the path of [un]truth.
> Come and see: A man should always attempt to study the Torah and its commandments even if he does not do so for its own sake, since from not doing it for its own sake he will come [to do it] for its own sake.[1]

We learn from this passage that even if the harm [caused by] error is great, it nonetheless appertains only to one who is unqualified to teach and [yet] teaches. However, [with regard to] the subject of teaching oneself, there is no harm at all stemming from error. On the contrary, [such a person] receives a reward—though not as great a reward as that [given to] one who arrives at the truth. The difference between them is similar to that between the barren tree and those trees which bear fruit. Thus holiness increases and bears fruit in the light which emanates from the true Torah of one who knows its secrets and continually teaches them. The same [holds] for the other divisions of the Torah. There is no doubt that [such a teacher] will cause an emanation, and that this emanation and light which is created [through the teaching] will abide forever, bearing fruit for himself and for generations [to come]. Thus it is written, *He keeps mercy to the thousandth generation* (Exod. 34:7). He retains [His] mercy to a thousand generations with regard to the merit of the fathers and similar things. The essence of the good deed, which constitutes the essence of the light, is kept for him for the world-to-come, where he sits and enjoys [it].

This is not the case with the barren tree, which does not bear fruit. The reason is that the *kelipah*[2] does not bear fruit. Thus [also]

1. Cf. Pesaḥim 50b.

2. The *kelipah* (lit. "shell") refers to those demonic forces which both stand in opposition to the sefirotic realm of holiness and derive their life-energy from it.

one who studies mistakenly necessarily inclines that study after the "outside" ones. Like the "outside" ones, he bears no fruit. They also surround the stream. The "stream" is Yesod, the locus of mysteries,[3] for "light" (*'or*) is [the numeric equivalent of] "mystery" (*raz*) This "light," which is stored away for the righteous,[4] departs, [for] *the secret of the Lord is to those who fear Him and His covenant* (Ps. 25:14). [*Covenant*] is Yesod, the secret of [the divine name] Yah.[5] In sum, [these] surround this stream [and] constitute a thin covering (*kelipah*), about which is written, *a brightness was round about it* (Ezek. 1:4). This constitutes the foreskin, which had been split and pulled down but not cut off, as has been explained.[6] It constitutes an aid, border, and covering for the tree that bears fruit. Thus the *willows of the stream* [16a] surround the stream, and there they benefit. Just so, those who err [in their study] form trees there in which the Holy One, blessed be He, rejoices, for ultimately these willows are useful and beautify the stream. They are bound together in the lulav.[7]

3. On the sefirah Yesod as "locus of mysteries," see Elliot Wolfson, "Circumcision, Vision of God and Textual Interpretation: From Midrashic Trope to Mystical Symbol", *History of Religions* 27 (1987): 189-215, esp. pp. 205-215; idem, "Circumcision and the Divine Name," *Jewish Quarterly Review* 78 (1987): 77-112, esp. 100-101, 103-106.

4. Cf. Zohar I, 31b-32a; II, 148b-149a.

5. See Wolfson, "Circumcision and the Divine Name."

6. In a ritual circumcision, there are two parts to the operation, the removal of the foreskin and the tearing (*periah*) of the mucous membrane. Without both operations, a Jewish circumcision is considered incomplete. The "brightness" is a reference to the *kelipah* called *nogah* ("brightness"), which occupies an intermediate position between the realms of the sefirot and the *kelipah*.

7. On the festival of Sukkot, the prayer ritual utilizes "four species"—the etrog (citron), lulav (palm branch), hadas (myrtle), and 'aravah (willow). The willow was considered the least important of the four, but nonetheless was needed for the set to be complete. See Lev. 23:40.

Would that we merit to have a portion even of those "willows," for all is for the beautification of the lulav. Thus it was said, *in its love you will be continually infatuated*, as we have explained. The willow certainly [is necessary to complete] the lulav.

Just as the "willows" surround the "stream," so is it impossible to reach the inside of the nut unless one enters by way of the shell (*kelipah*). Similarly, *the way to life is the rebuke that admonishes.* The "rebuke" constitutes the shell of the nut, which is definitely *the way to life.* May God grant us merit [to attain the level of] "fruit trees." It would [thus] be impossible for us not to achieve it.

From this passage it is also clear that even if a man cannot find someone who can teach him properly, he should not refrain for this reason from pursuing Torah, for in the end he will have reward for [his] study. Thus he will merit the truth, in contradiction to the opinion of the other groups we mentioned and discussed in chapter 3.

6

Having sufficiently discussed those who stand aloof from this science, and having refuted their opinion—as God has helped us—we will now explain how those who cultivate it should be motivated in order to be accepted by their Master. We say that we know of three groups of those who cultivate [Kabbalah]. One of these errs; one sins; and one is worthy.

The erring group is comprised of some people in our time who have no preparation in either Scripture, Mishnah, or Gemara[1] [and yet] pursue this science. There is no doubt that they are completely in error from several perspectives:

1. Never in their lives have they seen the light of *pilpul*.[2] They have deviated from the [straight] path and have taken up the way of the nonallegorical understanding of this science until [16b] they are nigh to the error of imagining physicality in heavenly beings.[3] This [error] has befallen them because they have not been sufficiently prepared [by their studies] and have [thus] followed the plain meaning of statements, thinking that they were not allegories.

1. The Talmud consists of the Mishnah, redacted in the third century C.E. in the Land of Israel, and the Gemara, an expansion of Mishnaic ideas which emerged from the rabbinical academies of the Land of Israel and Babylon in the third through the sixth century C.E.

2. *Pilpul* is a methodology of Talmud study which sought to resolve difficulties and contradictions in the text, real or apparent, through the use of conceptual and casuistic analysis. On *pilpul* as practiced in Cordovero's era, see Chaim Zalman Dimitrovsky, "On the Pilpulistic Method" [Hebrew], *Salo Wittmayer Baron Jubilee Volume* (Jerusalem, 1974), Hebrew sec., pp. 111-182.

3. On this issue, see Maimonides, *Mishneh Torah*, Hilkhot Yesodei ha-Torah, chaps. 1-2.

They did not get to the bottom of the matter. This has caused many students who are worthy [of studying Kabbalah] to distance themselves from it and overthrow its yoke, despising the way taken by these devotees. The slogan in the mouth [of this group] is that this science has no need of *pilpul* and questions. Thus they have closed the gates of understanding for themselves and walk in darkness.

2. It is well known from the *Tikkunim* that the order of progress in the science of our holy Torah is to master Scripture, then to master Mishnah, and then to master Kabbalah.[4] [Nonetheless, this group] has [seemingly] advanced to the mastery of Kabbalah without [previously having mastered] the ladder and the way of [progressive] steps.

Let no one who hears this surmise that we intend [to imply] by this that we have [ourselves] achieved these levels, God forbid. However, we have taken the path [in] which we would guide them. They ought to accustom themselves to some *pilpul* according to the preparation of their intellect, as well as some study of Gemara and Mishnah. They should [also] know the laws necessary for them [in their daily lives] in order to avoid the fate of the astrologer who gazes into the heavens and does not see the pit before him and winds up falling into a deep pit.[5] They should, therefore, be introduced to the laws [requisite] for upright conduct. On this [basis] they will merit to walk their path securely.

The sinful [group] are those who cultivate [Kabbalah] because they think of themselves as great sages whose only lack is [the mastery] of this science. In order that they be [considered] absolutely perfect in all [knowledge], they have decided to pursue this subject a bit. They rationalize their defect [by saying], "Shall an

4. *Tikkunei Zohar*, introduction, 1b.

5. This astrologer is the forerunner of the modern "absent-minded professor."

inferior person speak before a sage like [me] and [I] be unable to answer? After all, it is also [my] portion." On top of this [rationalization] they possess an inordinate amount [17a] of pride. Moreover, they do not study [Kabbalah] for its own sake. [To acquire] a bit of this science is the same in their eyes as [acquiring] a smattering of medicine, astronomy, logic, mathematics, and the other sciences. Of these and their like, the rabbis, their memory be a blessing, said in Bereshit Rabbah [1.5]:

> Rabbi Huna, in the name of Bar Kappara, opened [his discourse with the verse]:
> *Let the lying lips be dumb* (Ps. 31:19).
> Let them be bound, let them be made dumb, let them be silenced.
> Let them be bound:
> [As] it states, *Behold, we were binding sheaves in the field* (Gen. 37:7).[6]
> Let them be made dumb:
> This is as you might say, *who makes a man dumb or deaf* (Exod. 4:11).
> He will silence them: [the meaning is] as it appears.
> [*which speak arrogantly against the righteous*]:
> Those who say of the Righteous One who lives forever [things] that He withheld from the creatures.
> *With pride*:
> In order to lord it [over them] and say, "I am expounding the Account of Creation.
> [*and contempt*:] He demeans My glory!
> Thus said Rabbi Yose ben Ḥanina:
> Anyone who honors himself through the disgrace of his fellow has no portion in the world-to-come.

6. In Cordovero's citation, this verse was not in its proper order. I have restored the text according to J. Theodor and Ch. Albeck, *Midrash Bereshit Rabbah* (Jerusalem: Wahrman, 1965), vol. 1, p. 3.

How much more does this apply to the honor of God.
What is written afterwards?
Oh, how abundant is Your goodness which You have laid up for those who fear You (Ps. 31:20).
[To them] and not to those who despise Your majesty.[7]

Now [this passage] specifically deals with this group which exchanges its glory for disgrace. In place of [achieving] honor they start a conflagration. They abandon the ways of uprightness for the paths of darkness. They will be ashamed; poverty [of spirit] is their portion. God save us from them and their portion!

The worthy group consists of those who take the straight path and have a portion [in the mastery] of Scripture, a portion in Gemara and its laws, which we consider to be Mishnah, and a portion of this science [of Kabbalah].[8] They study it for its own sake in order to enter into its mysteries, to know their Master, and to achieve a wondrous level in the true acquisition of knowledge of the Torah. [They also study it in order] to pray before their Master and to unify, through their [performance of] His commandments, the Holy One, blessed be He, and His Shekhinah.[9] This is the preferred [method of] worshipping the Creator of all. I know truly that [such a person] will go on his way with security. When he lies down, he will not fear, for his Master will faithfully inform him [of matters] in the divine Torah that none who preceded him had attained. For each [17b] soul has a special portion in the Torah.

7. The last sentence is not contained in the standard edition of Bereshit Rabbah. It is to be found, however, in the *editio princeps* (Constantinople, 5272 [1512]), which Cordovero apparently used.

8. On the tripartite division of study, see Maimonides, *Mishneh Torah*, Hilkhot Talmud Torah 1:11-12.

9. This is a reference to the union of the sefirot Tiferet and Malkhut, which is a central image in Kabbalah.

There is no man who attained a limitless [knowledge] of all of it with the exception of Moses our rabbi, peace upon him. Moreover, the Holy One, blessed be He, did not inform even him [of the entire Torah] in its generalities and specifics [and] in the name of the sages [holding various] opinions and of their students who were to expound it, as, for example, "*Eleazar, my son, says, a yearling calf.*"[10]

Having saved the reader from [the influence of] arguments preventing him from pursuing this science and attaining the truth, we come to a brief second part, which is an exposition of the obligation [to study] it.

10. Cf. Mishnah, Parah 1:1. In the Mishnah, the text reads "Rabbi Eleazar said" and not "Eleazar, my son, says."

PART II

On the Obligation of the Enlightened
to Study Theology

1

There is no doubt that one of the things the Torah commands is for man to understand his Creator according to his intellectual level, as it is written, *I am the Lord your God* (Exod. 20:2, Deut. 5:6). Rabbi Moses ben Maimon dealt with this commandment at the beginning of his book (*Mishneh Torah*, Yesodei ha-Torah 1.1):

> The foundation of foundations and the pillar of the sciences is to know that there exists a First Cause which brought into being all that exists in heaven and earth.

We need cite no farther. There can be no doubt that the intention of Rabbi [Moses] was to include in this commandment [the command] to understand the order of being [stemming] from Him [as far as] human understanding [can comprehend]. This can be proven from the length of his explanation of this matter, [which encompasses] two entire paragraphs.[1] It is also included in his brief statement. When he said, "to know that there exists a First Cause which brought into being all that exists," [he indicated that] one needs to know as well the order of the bringing of the existents into being. He also specified the scriptural verse *I am the Lord your God*, meaning, "you must ascertain concerning Me, the Lord, [that I am] your God." [18a] This refers to Providence, which [extends] from the highest beings to the creation of lowly man. There is no doubt about this, for how is it possible to understand the word *to*

1. Maimonides, *Mishneh Torah*, Hilkhot Yesodei ha-Torah 2:2, 12. Cf. *Guide of the Perplexed*, introduction and 3.28.

know [except to assert] that it indicates belief in the existence of God? This being so, he should have stated, "[It is] a positive commandment to believe that God exists." [However,] he did not state this, but rather [utilized the wording] *to know that there exists.* Evidently, [then, this commandment] requires the acquisition of actual knowledge concerning God according to the power of the human intellect. Thus Scripture states, *Know the God of your father and serve Him* (I Chron. 28:9). [This verse] teaches that in order to serve [God] properly one needs [to acquire] knowledge concerning Him—that is, knowledge of His sefirot, His conduct with them, and His unification with them.[2] That is proper worship, [which causes] the unification of the Holy One, blessed be He, and His Shekhinah. That is why [the verse] specifies *and serve him* (*va-'avadahu*), which signifies *and serve hu* (i.e., *heh vav,* indicating] the Holy One, blessed be He, and His Shekhinah.

When [Scripture] states *know,* it is similar to [its use in] *Adam knew Eve, his wife* (Gen. 4:1). *The God of your father* refers to [the sefirah] Malkhut, the soul of David. Alternatively, *God* refers to Malkhut [and] *your father* [to] Jacob,[3] father of Solomon, who is in Yesod. Thus *and serve him,* as has been explained.

He thus explained this verse: *Did your father not eat and drink and do justice and righteousness? Then it was well with him. He judged the cause of the poor and needy. Then it was well. Is this not to know Me? says the Lord* (Jer. 22:15-16). It means that the unification of the Holy One, blessed be He, and His Shekhinah—which is what David and the other proper kings did—is signified [by the

2. The nature of God's relationship with the sefirot was the subject of debate among Kabbalists. Was God co-extensive with the sefirot, or did they constitute instruments which He utilized? In his analysis of this problem, Cordovero tended to hedge his bets somewhat. See Yosef Ben-Shlomo, *The Mystical Theology of Moses Cordovero* [Hebrew] (Jerusalem: Mossad Bialik, 1986), chap. 2.

3. The reference is to Tiferet.

terms] *justice and righteousness.* Naturally, *then it was well with him. Well* signifies [the sefirah Yesod]. Similarly, *he judged the cause of the poor and needy* [refers] to the [sefirotic] levels of Yesod and Malkhut, which are [termed] "poor and needy."[4] When man judges their cause in this lowly world, He changes them to mercy in the upper world. This is [the significance of] *Is not this to know Me? says the Lord,* for by this the Holy One, blessed be He, achieves union with His Shekhinah.

Now these reparations [cannot come about] except through the persistent study of [Kabbalistic] science with the proper intent [as well as] the observance of the commandments, Torah [study], and prayer. Then, certainly, the Holy One, blessed be He, and His Shekhinah will unite and perfect [man's] worship and [his] grasp of these matters which [truly] constitute [18b] knowledge.

The intent of our [non-Kabbalist] predecessors is [partially] correct and near to this subject, except that they did not take the path of the sefirot [but rather dealt with God's] providence over the spheres according to their understanding.[5] Rabbi Moses ben Maimon himself stated this in the previously mentioned chapter.[6]

> This existent is the God of the universe, Lord over all the world. It is He who conducts [the motion of the] sphere with a force which has no end or limit or interruption. For the sphere turns continually, and it is impossible that it should turn without a turner. He, blessed be He, turns it with neither hand nor body. Knowledge of this matter is a positive commandment, as it is written, *I am the Lord your God.*

4. They are "poor and needy" because they receive the flow of divine energy from the higher sefirot.

5. Cordovero, in *Elimah Rabbati* 1.16, stated that "In matters metaphysical, oftentimes the true masters of Cabala will be found to agree with the philosophers." Cited in Harry A. Wolfson, *The Philosophy of Spinoza* (Cambridge, Mass.: Harvard University Press, 1934), vol. 1, p. 17.

6. Maimonides, *Mishneh Torah*, Hilkhot Yesodei ha-Torah 1:5.

Here he explained that the knowledge of the motion of the spheres with divine force and direction constitutes this positive commandment. If this is so, then no Israelite should neglect to acquire this [knowledge] according to its fundamentals, each according to his capacity. The beginning of knowledge in these matters [consists] in general in these findings. Afterwards one may increase his observance of this commandment according to the greatness of his intelligence and knowledge.

2

Beside this there are other commandments which cannot be properly fulfilled without knowledge of Torah and of this wondrous science. These [commandments] are the love and fear of God. They are commandments addressed to us in the Torah. [Concerning] love, it is written, *You will love the Lord your God* (Deut. 6:5). [Of] fear it is written, *You will fear the Lord your God* (Deut. 6:13, 10:20). If one does not comprehend the awesome majesty of His divinity, His separation from the rest of the existents, the origin of all that exists from Him as well as the number of degrees which exist until [His] providence reaches this lowly world, how can one fear Him?

The poor man thinks that God is an old man, as it is written, *the ancient of days sits*; that he has white hair because of His great age, as it is written, *the hair of his head like pure wool*; and [that] He sits on a marvelous throne of fire which gives off flashes, as it is written, *His throne was fiery flames* (Dan. 7:9). [He thinks that] His appearance is similar to fire, as it is written, *For the Lord your God is a consuming* [19a] *fire* (Deut. 4:24, 9:3). There are other, similar fantasies which the fool believes in his mind, so that he anthropomorphizes God and [thus] falls into one of the traps which destroy [one's] faith. His fear [of God] increases only on account of his imagination.[1]

In contradistinction [to this fool], the enlightened sage will know God's unity and complete separation from bodily categories. He would not, God forbid, ascribe these to Him. He would not

1. Cf. Maimonides, *Mishneh Torah*, Hilkhot Yesodei ha-Torah 1:9; idem, *Guide of the Perplexed* 2.13 ff.

even ascribe such things to the least of His attendants, for the ninth sphere marks the cessation of corporeality. He would be amazed and astonished [at this fool] and say, "Who am I? I am as a mustard seed in relation to the sphere of the moon, and that is as a mustard seed in relation to the second sphere. This is also the relationship of the second sphere and all it contains in relation to the third sphere. This [is the relationship] of all of them—one inside the other—like a mustard seed in relation to the rest of the firmaments, as is explained in the chapters on the Account of Creation [composed] by our rabbis, their memory be a blessing.[2] And all of these are like a mustard seed in relation to the firmaments described in the Chapters of the [Account of the] Chariot [composed] by our rabbis, their memory be a blessing."[3]

From this [realization], his fear [of God] will strengthen. He will feel himself to be lowly and obscure, and will say to himself, "Who am I before these great servants of my Creator?" Thus he will utterly fear [God's] majesty. With this, great love [of God] will be added to his soul, and he will die in communion [with God].[4] His soul, too, will be negated when he remembers [God's] statement: *I loved you, says the Lord* (Mal. 1:2). Thus he will perfect the commandment of love and fear [of God]. Without this, he will be unable to perfect himself [in the observance] of these commandments. In the Zohar, section Bereshit, similar things are explained.[5]

2. I have not been able to identify a composition entitled *Pirkei Ma'aseh Bereshit*; it is entirely likely that the reference here is to a genre of literature rather than a specific text. For a listing of works of this nature dealing with creation, such as *Baraita de-Ma'aseh Bereshit*, see Scholem, *Kabbalah*, p. 375.

3. *Pirkei Heikhalot* is the medieval name for *Heikhalot Rabbati*. See Scholem, *Kabbalah*, p. 374. For an English translation of portions of this work, see David Blumenthal, *Understanding Jewish Mysticism* (New York: Ktav, 1978), vol. 1, pp. 56-90.

4. On *devekut*, see Scholem, *Kabbalah*, pp. 174-176. Cf. Idel, *Kabbalah*, pp. 35 ff.

5. Cf. Zohar I, 11b-12a.

[19b]

PART III

On the Manner and Time of Study

1

The Time of Study

I have seen fit to divide this subject into three parts. The first concerns a person's preparation in order to be worthy to enter the palace.[1] For it is improper for anyone "who comes to fill his hands . . . and dress in the priestly vestments to serve in the place of holiness" [cf. Exod. 29:29] to come and dress himself, God forbid. On the contrary, it is fitting for him to first strip from himself the shell of gross pride which prevents him from attaining the truth. He should [then] direct his heart to heaven [to pray] that he should not fail and be counted among the sinners referred to in chapter 6 of part I.

Secondly, he must be accustomed to engaging in profound *pilpul* so that he might be ready and able to separate [relevant] matters from parables. Then he will reach the desired goal in this science.

Thirdly, he must apply himself to fill his belly with [the study of] the laws of the Gemara and the explanation of the commandments on the literal level in the work of Rabbi Moses ben Maimon, the *Yad*.[2]

1. Cf. Maimonides, *Guide of the Perplexed* 3.51.

2. The reference is to Maimonides' *Mishneh Torah*. In his introduction to that work, Maimonides states that one of the reasons he wrote it was to allow Jews to fulfill their obligation of Torah study in a relatively short time so as to enable them to study philosophical issues. Cordovero here seems to take up this notion and transfer it to the study of Kabbalah.

Fourthly, he should also guide himself [in the study of] Scripture, whether [it be] much or little, in order to complete [his mastery of] Scripture, Mishnah, and correct knowledge.[3] [Then] he will not fail and be [counted with] the erring group I discussed in [part I] chapter 6.

Afterwards he should purify his thoughts from the vanities and pleasures of the moment to the extent that this is possible in our time.[4] Then, surely, the gates of wisdom will be opened for him.

Let the reader not think that these instructions are [mere] advice and spurn them, for they are correct and relevant, and based upon foundations of pure gold—the words of our rabbis, their memory be a blessing, in several places.

The second [division of this subject] concerns the proper time [for study]. There is no doubt that it is improper for one to commence [the study of] this science if he has not married a woman and purified his thoughts.[5] Do not answer me [with examples of] some who have studied [esoteric lore] in previous [20a] times, for not all minds are equal.

Also, [the student] has to have reached at least [his] twentieth year in order to have achieved at least half the age of "understanding."[6] Though some have stated [that this study should not be undertaken] until he reaches his fortieth year,[7] we disagree. Many have acted in accordance with our opinion and succeeded.

3. Cf. *Mishneh Torah*, Hilkhot Talmud Torah 1:11-12.

4. Cordovero subscribed to the notion prevalent in rabbinic literature that each generation is lesser in stature than the one which preceded it.

5. Marriage was supposed to settle the mind because after marrying one would not be disturbed by unsatisfied sexual desires.

6. In his introduction to *Pardes Rimmonim*, Cordovero indicates that he himself was introduced to the study of Kabbalah at the age of twenty.

7. On the notion that Kabbalah study should not be commenced prior to the age of forty, see Moshe Idel, "On the History of the Interdiction Against the Study of Kabbalah Before the Age of Forty" [Hebrew], *AJS Review* 5 (1980): 1-20 (Hebrew pagination).

All this having been said, everything depends upon [one's] purity of heart, as I have mentioned, and upon the quality of the advice [received]. This is hinted at in several places in the Zohar, where they stated, "Until you have cooked your cooking."[8]

The third [division] concerns the proper time for learning. It is certainly easy for a person to study throughout the day. However, the optimum time for gaining profound wisdom is the long night, from midnight on,[9] or on the Sabbath day, which is [itself] a factor. Thus also the eve of the Sabbath commencing at noontime and on holidays, particularly on 'Aẓeret.[10] I have tried this many times and found it to be a marvelously successful day. Also, there is great success [in studying] on Sukkot in the sukkah. These times [I have] mentioned I have tried. I am speaking from experience.

8. Cf. Zohar II, 29a. The phrase in its context means that thought must mature before pronouncements are made.

9. On the phenomenon of midnight prayer in Kabbalah, see among other texts, Zohar II, 195b-196b, 205a; III, 23a, 171b-172a, 302a. Cf. also Scholem, "Tradition and New Creation in the Ritual of the Kabbalists," *On the Kabbalah and Its Symbolism* (New York: Schocken, 1965), pp. 118-157, and Elliot Horowitz, "Coffee, Coffeehouses and the Nocturnal Rituals of Early Modern Jewry," *AJS Review* 14 (1989): 17-46.

10. 'Aẓeret refers to the festival of Shavuot. Cf. Mishnah, Rosh ha-Shanah 1:2, Ḥagigah 2:4. Cf. Yehuda Liebes, "Ha-Mashiaḥ shel ha-Zohar," for a discussion of the Zoharic traditions concerning the preparation of the Shekhinah for her marriage with the Holy One, one of the bases of the custom of *tikkun leyl shavuot*.

2

The Manner of Study

[In his study,] the student must combine fear and joy, as it is written, *rejoice with trembling* (Ps. 2:11). [He must] add modesty to these two virtues. The reason for the combination of these three virtues [is this]: He requires [the virtue of] fear lest he err and sin. Moreover, he is delving [in his studies] in the place of the flame of the fire of joy, which matter, I have heard, requires prayer [for success]. Also, the Torah certainly depends upon [the virtue of] joy.

Modesty is most important. [The student] should say, "Who am I? What is my life that I should pursue the mysteries of the divine Torah which the Holy One, blessed be He, has hidden from flesh and blood?" Moreover, who can speak of the qualities of the king, while the king is listening, and not be ashamed?

I almost believe that one must add to these three [qualities] regret for one's spoiled youth[1] and for the various activities [20b] which constitute a divisive barrier [to esoteric knowledge]. In the book of *Tikkunim* they stated explicitly that sin is a shell [which prevents] the intellect from comprehending the esoteric.[2] [Thus] when a halakhah escapes the enlightened [Kabbalist], he must occupy himself with the commandments, which are from the right [side],[3] and then he will grasp the mystery. This is the essence of

1. Cordovero states this regret with regard to himself in his introduction to *Pardes Rimmonim*.

2. *Tikkunei Zohar*.

3. The reference is to the "right side" of the sefirotic structure, which is the side of mercy and holiness.

their statement. We have learned from this and are accustomed [to the practice] that when one fulfills a commandment and then goes to pursue the esoteric, that which had been difficult becomes revealed.

Also, a man should continually confess [his] sins with a broken heart. This certainly helps overcome the *kelipah*.[4]

We have found a discussion of some of these matters [in the Zohar,] section Naso at the beginning of the *'Idra*[5] (Zohar III, 127b-128a).

It was taught:
Rabbi Simeon said to the colleagues:
"How long will we sit in a place of one pillar?
As it is written:
It is time to act for the Lord (Ps. 119:126).
'The days are short and the lender presses' (Avot 5:9).
All day the [divine] decree cries out,
and they that harvest the field are few.
They are the 'ripe' [grapes] of the vineyard, and they do not look and do not know properly where they are going.
Enter, O colleagues, into the threshing floor (*'idra*),
dressed in armor and [bearing] spears.
Hurry your preparations in counsel, in wisdom,
in understanding, and in knowledge,
with sight, with [strength] of hands and feet.
Make king over you He who has life and death in His power.
[That He may] decree words of truth, words which the higher holy ones hear and are glad to hear and know."
Rabbi Simeon sat and wept and said:

4. A reference to the forces of evil.

5. For an interesting analysis of the *'Idra*, see Yehuda Liebes, "Ha-Mashiaḥ shel ha-Zohar," *The Messianic Idea in Jewish Thought* (Jerusalem, 1977), pp. 87-236.

"Woe [to me] if I reveal [this], and woe [to me] if I do not reveal."
The colleagues who were present were silent.
Rabbi Abba arose and said:
"If it pleases you, sir, [to reveal this matter] it is written, *The secret of the Lord is to those who fear Him* (Ps. 25:14).
Now the colleagues do fear the Holy One, blessed be He.
They have already entered the *'idra* concerning the Tabernacle.[6]
Some entered and some left."
It was taught:
The colleagues were numbered in front of Rabbi Simeon.
Present were his son, Rabbi Eleazar, Rabbi Abba, Rabbi Judah, Rabbi Yose bar Jacob, Rabbi Isaac bar Hezekiah bar Rav, Rabbi Yose, and Rabbi Yessa.
They presented their hands to Rabbi Simeon and straightened their fingers.
They entered a field among trees and sat.
Rabbi Simeon arose [21a] and said:
"Let everyone place his hand on my breast."
They placed their hands, and he took them.
He commenced:
"*Cursed be the man who will make an idol and a graven image* (Deut. 27:15)."
Rabbi Simeon opened [his discourse]:
"*It is time to act for the Lord. They have made void your Torah.*

Why *is it time to act for the Lord*?
Because *they have made void your Torah*.
What is [the meaning of] *they have made void your Torah*?
It refers to the upper Torah,[7] which is voided if it is not observed properly.

6. Zohar II, 127a-146a.
7. A reference to the sefirah Ḥokhmah or Binah.

Of the ancient of days[8] it was said:
Happy are you, O Israel, who is like you? (Deut. 33:29).
It is further written:
Who is like you, O Lord? (Exod. 15:11)."
He called Rabbi Eleazar, his son, and seated him in front of him.
Rabbi Abba was on the other side.
He said:
"We are the sum of all.
Up to now, the pillars have been established."
They were silent.
They heard a sound, and their knees knocked together.
What was that sound?
It was the sound of the Assembly on High gathering.
Rabbi Simeon rejoiced and said:
"*O Lord, I have heard your report and am afraid* (Hab. 3:2).
There it is proper to be fearful.
We [, however,] depend upon love.
Thus it is written:
You will love your fellow as yourself (Lev. 19:18).
You will love the Lord your God (Deut. 6:5, 11:1).
And *I have loved you, says the Lord* (Mal. 1:2)."

From this passage it is clear that one requires great fear [of God to pursue] this science, particularly when one deals with the *shi'ur komah*.[9] One also requires love [of God]. I have heard that the ancients used to sit upon the earth when teaching this science to students in order to make them [feel] humility and awe. This is proven in "The Secret of the Beard and Its Hair."[10] I have also found some support for this in the Zohar, section Aḥarei Mot [III, 59b].

8. A reference to the sefirah Keter.
9. On *shi'ur komah*, lit. the "measurement of [God's] body," see Scholem, *Kabbalah*, pp. 16-18.
10. Zohar III, 59b.

Rabbi Simeon and the colleagues went to the house of Rabbi Pinḥas.
They went until they arrived at the house of Rabbi Pinḥas.
Rabbi Pinḥas went out and kissed him.
He said, "We have merited to kiss the Shekhinah.
Goodly is my portion!"
He entered his house and made couches with awnings.
Rabbi Simeon said, "The Torah does not require this."
He removed them and they sat.

This is close to what has been said.

[21b]

3

From Whom Shall [the Student] Learn?

Previous [indications] in this matter [are] that one may not study Torah except from a *messenger of the Lord of Hosts* (Mal. 2:7), as our rabbis, their memory be a blessing, have taught.[1] They have also said that one should not learn from a magus.[2] Besides that, there are two rules [to be followed] by those beginning in this science.

[The first is] that they should not study except with one who has conducted himself according to the principles I have outlined up to this point. This excludes [members of] the "erring" and "sinning" groups.[3] One should not learn from them, for I guarantee that [this science] will not be found among them at all. Moreover, [the student] would be [placing himself] in grave danger of losing his faith, for we have seen many men erring in many [of these] matters because they followed [the opinions of] these groups.

[Secondly,] he should attempt to study with one who has conducted himself as uprightly as possible, for in his hands are entrusted the treasuries of his Master. Let [the student] not chase after those who boast of their knowledge, for while their voices sound like the waves of the sea, they [actually] contain not even a fourth [of a *log* of wisdom]. I have experienced this many times.

The same [caveat] applies to some authors who compose their books with riddles and metaphors and rhymes so that their mes-

1. Mo'ed Katan 17a: "If the master is like a 'messenger of God,' they should seek Torah from his mouth. If not, let them not seek Torah from his mouth."

2. Shabbat 75a: "He who learns one thing from a magus is worthy of death."

sage is encumbered by much [extraneous] matter. We ourselves would not do this, God forbid. It is improper to place a blemish on sanctified things.

These are the books which one should stick to; [reading] them is praiseworthy. They are the compositions of Rabbi Simeon bar Yoḥai, peace upon him, such as the Zohar, the *Tikkunim*, *Ra'aya Mehemna*, *Shir ha-Shirim*, *Sabba*, and *Yanuka*.[3] [Of the books of Rabbi Simeon's] predecessors, [one can find] Sefer *Yeẓirah*,[4] the *Bahir*,[5] Midrash Ruth and Midrash Lamentations from the Zohar.[6] From [his] successors [one can find] the Midrash of the Scroll of Esther from the Zohar.[7] Also [there is] the book *Ma'ayan ha-Ḥokhmah*, the Chapters of the Chariot, the Chapters of the Account of Creation, and similar works,[8] [as well as] a few minor works of Rabbi Simeon bar Yoḥai, peace upon him. [The student] should stick with these works lovingly, and he will [then] succeed in [mastering] this science on condition that he delve deeply into them and [devote to them] exceptional study. He will then find explanations for most of what is to be found in the books of the

3. These are some different sections of the Zohar. For a complete listing of these sections, see Scholem, *Major Trends*, pp. 159-163.

4. *Sefer Yeẓirah* was attributed to the patriarch Abraham. Cf. Scholem, *Kabbalah*, pp. 23-30.

5. *Sefer ha-Bahir* was attributed to R. Neḥunya b. ha-Kanah. Cf. Scholem, *Kabbalah*, pp. 312-316.

6. It is noteworthy that Cordovero considers these two works, normally associated with the Zoharic literature, to have emanated from a time prior to that of Rabbi Simeon bar Yoḥai, putative author of the Zohar.

7. To date, no section of the Zohar proper dealing with Esther has been found. Cf. Scholem, *Kabbalah*, p. 219.

8. These texts, with the exception of *Ma'ayan ha-Ḥokhmah*, which I have been unable to identify, are texts of *Merkavah* mysticism. Cf. Scholem, *Kabbalah*, pp. 373-376. The work referred to as *Ma'ayan ha-Ḥokhmah* might be either the introduction to the magical text *Shimmushei Torah*, published by Jellinek in *Bet ha-Midrasch* 1, pp. 58-65, or, perhaps, one of the texts of the *'Iyyun* circle.

latter commentators, which he need not consult. [22a] It is not our intention to declare these [latter works] unfit, God forbid, but rather to indicate for the [would-be] student the path which is short, though it seems to be long.[9]

The reader should approach these books in two ways. First of all, he should review the texts many times, making notes in order to remember [his] studies fluently. He should not delve too deeply at first. Secondly, he should study the material with great concentration according to his ability. Thus the reader should have two permanent rules: (1) [To study] with concentration at the times mentioned in [part III] chapter 1. (2) [To study] with fluency according to his ability. At times [the proportions] should be increased and sometimes lessened, all according to the need of the hour and the [degree of] peace of mind. Thus [the student] shall go on his way confident of attaining the straight path.

Though it may seem to the student that he does not understand [the material], he should nevertheless not cease studying, for his Master will faithfully cause him to discover esoteric wisdom. For just as a father trains his son, so does the Holy One, blessed be He, grant merit to one who pursues this science bit by bit. I have experienced this innumerable times. There is proof for this course [of action] from the Zohar [passage] I cited in part I, chapter 5, with God's help.

9. A similar tendency to disregard later Kabbalistic works can be found in a passage from the introduction to *Sha'ar ha-Hakdamot*, attributed to R. Ḥayyim Vital and printed at the beginning of *Etz Ḥayyim* and *Sefer Oẓrot Ḥayyim*. It states that the founders of Kabbalah, from R. Abraham b. David to Naḥmanides, received true Kabbalah from the revelation of the prophet Elijah. However, the Kabbalistic works after Naḥmanides, according to the fragment, should not be read, since they were based on human intellect and were not received either from earlier authorities or from heavenly beings (*'elyonim*). Cf. Elliot Wolfson, "By Way of Truth," p. 105, n. 6.

Should any subject in this science seem doubtful for [the student], he should wait, for in the course of time the matter will be revealed to him. The essential reward [for the study] of this science is [derived from] waiting for [the revelation of] the mysteries which will be revealed to him in the course of time. In several passages in the Zohar it is proven that oftentimes something which had been doubtful for them for a long time would come to them. Their saying was "We have searched all day for this word."[10] This is [also proven] in [Zohar,] section Ḥayyei Sarah, [where it states that the verse *who works*] *for Him waits for Him* (Isa. 64:3) was written for this [context].[11] We will cite [this] further on in part IV, chapter 3. Moreover, often [the student's] knowledge of the treatises he previously [studied] will increase with the passage of time. [Something] similar is to be found in the Zohar.

It occurs to those who succeed in this science, that when they search these treatises many times, their knowledge will increase. In a similar context we say, There is no investigation without new [knowledge resulting].

10. I have not succeeded in identifying this passage from the Zohar.
11. Zohar I, 130b.

[22b]

4

How One Should Conduct Oneself [in Order] to Teach This Science to Others

One may not teach [this science] except to a person who serves God in cleanliness and purity. The following is found in the *Tikkunim*:[1]

> One must reveal deep mysteries to those who possess these good qualities.
>
> However, he who reveals mysteries [of the Torah] to the wicked, it is as if he revealed the genitals of the Torah for the sons of Lilith, the evil maidservant, mother of the wicked evil multitude.[2]
>
> He who reveals to them the secrets of the Torah causes the departure of the flow [of emanation] from the righteous Yesod, of whom it is said, *The secret of the Lord is for those who fear Him* (Ps. 25:14), and from the Shekhinah, as it is written, *The water left the sea, and the river is dry and parched* (Job. 14:11). At that time, the righteous below are entirely impoverished: bereft of the mysteries of Torah and poor in their bodies.
>
> Those who reveal mysteries to the righteous cause the "righteous" [Yesod] and the Shekhinah enlightenment in the mysteries of the Torah, for "light' (*or*) and "mystery" (*raz*) are [numerically] equivalent.[3]

1. This passage is not to be found in the *Tikkunei Zohar*. It is found in *Zohar Hadash* (ed. Margaliot), 94b.

2. Lilith is the "queen" of the domain of evil.

3. Both are equivalent to 207 in gematria, the sum of the numerical equivalent of their letters.

> At that time, *the enlightened will shine like the splendor of the firmament* (Dan. 12:13).

This is all [we need to cite] for our purpose. [However,] the [following] points must be made:

1. They stated, "However, he who reveals mysteries [of the Torah] to the wicked," and afterwards stated, "He who reveals to them . . . causes . . . the righteous." Why did [the passage] not say "reveals the genitals of the Torah," as was stated above? Alternatively, let it say in the first instance "causes the Righteous." Why are there two differing [versions]?

2. It states, "causes." However, the word "causes" is not exact. It ought to have stated, "makes the righteous," for this is the very one who causes damage above.

3. "At that time the righteous below." What is the reason for all this exposition?

The remaining linguistic points will be covered in the commentary, with God's help.

The reason that [the passage] declared, "Those who possess these qualities" is that they denote people in possession of the qualities of the righteous kings, seers, [and] prophets, masters of Torah, heroes [who are] pious, understanding, [and] wise; chiefs of the thousands of Israel. It was stated there that [the secrets of Torah] must be revealed to those who are the embodiment of these [sefirotic] qualities, occupy themselves with the commandments related to them, and whose souls are emanated from [23a] them. In other words there exists an obligation for one [who knows] to reveal the deep mysteries to them. In order to prove this obligation on the part of the knowledgeable person to teach one who fears [God], [the author] dealt with the opposite [situation] and derived the [positive] commandment from the prohibition [against teaching one who does not possess these qualities]. [The passage] states, "However, he who reveals mysteries [of the Torah] to the wicked," meaning that he reveals "the genitals of the Torah." In other words, Torah is [the sefirah] Tiferet. He who spreads the mysteries of the Torah among the wicked sins. For through Tiferet he spreads it to the "outside" ones, God forbid.[4] All the power of the wicked derives from the *kelipot.* Thus he who teaches him teaches the *kelipot*! This [teacher] spreads the mysteries of the Torah, which is Tiferet, and thus reveals the nakedness of the Torah "for the sons of . . . the maidservant." The intention is to demonstrate how the wicked and the *kelipah* are as one, and though the wicked is the son of Lilith, the evil maidservant, it is all one—mother and children. For the soul of the wicked and the strength of his wickedness stem from his mother, the maidservant. Thus we have demonstrated how the king [Tiferet] strengthens and influences the "maidservant." That is the meaning of "genitals of the Torah." He who reveals mysteries [of the Torah] to the wicked actually does this!

As well, he has caused another action, "the departure of the flow [of emanation] from Yesod." Because the king is cohabiting with the "maidservant" [Lilith], God forbid, he does not consort with the "mistress" [Malkhut]. It is thus accepted that [the wicked teacher] causes the removal of the flow [of emanation] from Tiferet to Yesod, since [Tiferet] is doing nothing other than cohabiting with the "outside" ones. Thus it would appear that he could not consort with the "inner" ones, the righteous Yesod, God forbid.

All this teaches that the mysteries of the Torah abide in Yesod. Thus [the sefirah] is called Yesod, [a combination of] the *yod* of the

4. Evil gets its power from the same divine source as the sefirot. Since it would not derive power from divine emanation in the ordinary course of events, it must contrive to "steal" power from the sefirotic system, the rightful recipient.

covenant and mystery [*sod*], which is the mystery of the Torah. Proof for this is [derived from the verse], *The secret of the Lord is for those who fear Him; and His covenant to make them know it* (Ps. 25:14). Thus "covenant" and "mystery" are as one. All this demonstrates that when mysteries [of the Torah] are spread among the "outside" ones, they are removed from the "inner" ones.

"The departure of the flow [of emanation] [23b] from [Yesod]." Thus the source of Yesod, which is Tiferet, removes itself, as has been explained. Since there is no [flow of] emanation in Yesod, he does not consort with Malkhut, as was said.

"And from the Shekhinah." The proof from Scripture is *the water left the sea.* This means that the reason for the lack of water in the sea, which is Malkhut, is because the river, which is Yesod, *is dry and parched.* This proves that during the time that the "river" is dry, there can be no water in the "sea," for it can receive no influx except through Yesod. Thus when [Tiferet] is separated from Yesod, it is likewise separated from the Shekhinah.

"At that time the righteous below." A difficulty [which might be posed] is that [the passage] stated that because [the teacher] reveals mysteries [of the Torah] to the wicked, *the river is dry,* indicating that there will be no emanation at all. However, this is not exact. [The passage should] rather [state] that there will be no mysteries [to be found] in Malkhut since that [teacher] spread the mysteries to the "outside." Why, then, should not the remaining [sefirotic] degrees of emanation receive their influx? That [possible difficulty] is why [the passage] specified "the departure of the flow," indicating that there is no emanation at all. There is proof [from this passage] that there is no emanation or flow at all. [This situation] is caused by those people below who are impoverished both in body and in the mysteries of Torah. This indicates the absolute removal of emanation. They are thus absolutely impoverished.

After [the passage] dealt with the sin of one who reveals [mysteries] to the wicked, one can understand the opposite—the eminence of the righteous, *for also this opposite, that did God make* (Eccles. 7:14). [Thus] "those who reveal mysteries to the righteous cause the righteous." By revealing the mystery to the righteous, [the teacher] causes emanation from the source on high, which is Tiferet, to Yesod. Thereupon Yesod clarifies these mysteries [in passing them] to Malkhut. This is [why the passage] states "cause the righteous," which is Yesod, "enlightenment in the mysteries of the Torah," which is the mystery of the emanation from Tiferet, termed "Torah," to the Shekhinah. This is its path.

[The passage] states "cause" and not "enlighten" because what is happening is that the "righteous" himself enlightens [24a] the aspect of [one] who is righteous like him.

Indeed "enlightenment in the mysteries of the Torah," from Tiferet to Malkhut, is caused naturally, since a good quality increases and spreads of itself.

"Light and mystery." This is problematic, because "mystery" rightly resides in Yesod, as was proven above. [However,] if this is true, how can these "mysteries" [also] stem from Tiferet? This [question] is why [the passage] stated that "light," which certainly resides in Tiferet, is called "mystery" [*raz*] and is numerically equivalent to "light" [*or*]. Therefore "mystery" can reside in Tiferet, except that in Tiferet it resides in the recondite aspect of "light," which is subtle, whereas in Yesod it partakes of the aspect of secret, which is more open and [able to be] revealed through the process of emanation.

The fact is that the [sefirah] Binah, which is above Tiferet, consists of one light. Binah influences the *vav* [of the Tetragrammaton] in the mystery of *resh*, which is Malkhut, the beginning [*reshit*] of the lower [beings]. Since the eminence of the revealer of mysteries is so great, he is obliged to entreat the "righteous" to reveal his secrets to him. This is [the meaning of] what was said at the beginning of the passage above, "One must reveal deep mysteries to those." The phrasing implies necessity and obligation, as is known.

From this passage, behold the punishment of one who reveals secrets to an unworthy person as well as the eminence of one who reveals them to a worthy student.

5

I have also found this in the Zohar, section 'Emor:[1]

Rabbi Ḥiyya opened his discourse:

"*Lord, when You went forth out of Seir; when You marched out of the field of Edom, the earth trembled, the heavens also dropped* (Judg. 5:4).
Come and see.
Worthy are Israel in this world and in the world-to-come, for the Holy One, blessed be He, delights in them, and they cling to Him and are called holy ones, the nation of God, until He caused them to rise to a high degree which is called 'holy,' as is written, *Holy is Israel to the Lord* (Jer. 2:3).
This is like that which we have taught.
For from eight days[2] Israel clings to Him [24b] through His Name and they are His, called by His Name below, as it is written, *And who is like Your people, Israel, a unique nation on earth?* (II Sam. 7:23, I Chron. 17:21).
The other [nations] do not cling to Him and do not follow His laws.
The holy engraving is turned from them until they cling to the 'other side,' which is not holy.
Come and see: When the Holy One, blessed be He, wished to give the Torah to Israel, He [first] invited the sons of Esau.[3]
He said to them, 'Do you with to accept My Torah?'

1. Zohar III, 91a-b. Cf. Elliot Wolfson, "Circumcision and the Divine Name," pp. 98, 103-105.

2. The reference is to circumcision, which is performed on the eighth day of life.

3. Cf. 'Avodah Zarah 2b.

At that time, the Holy Land quaked and desired to go into the pit of the great abyss.
It said before him, 'Master of the universe, shall the object of [your] love for the two thousand years prior to the creation of the world[4] come to those who are not included in Your covenant?
The Holy One, blessed be He, said to it, 'O Seat! O Seat![5]
The covenant of the holy Torah will not come before them, as it is written, *O Lord, when You left Seir, when You marched from the field of Edom, the earth quaked.*'
Certainly the Torah, which is a holy covenant, will be given only to one who possesses a holy covenant.
He who grants the Torah to one who has not entered into the holy covenant falsifies two covenants.
He falsifies the covenant of the Torah, and he falsifies the covenant between the 'righteous' [Yesod] and the community of Israel, for the Torah was given for that place and not another."[6]
Rabbi Abba said, "He falsifies three high places.
He falsifies the Torah, falsifies the Prophets, falsifies the Hagiographa.
He falsifies the Torah, as is written, *This is the Torah which Moses placed before the children of Israel* (Deut. 4:44).
He falsifies the Prophets, as it is written, *All your children shall be learned of the Lord* (Isa. 54:13)—[yours] and not [those of] another!
It is [also] written, 'seal up the Torah among My disciples'—[among] them and not others.
He falsifies the Hagiographa, as it is written, *For He established a testimony in Jacob and appointed a Torah in Israel* (Isa. 8:16).
It is also written, *Surely the righteous shall give thanks to Your Name* (Ps. 78:5).

4. Cf. Bereshit Rabbah 1:4.
5. The reference is to Malkhut.
6. "That place" signifies the covenant of circumcision. "Another" refers to the uncircumcised.

Who are these 'righteous'?
It is the righteous [Yesod] and the community of Israel [Malkhut]. He who has not entered into their covenant will not give thanks to His holy Name, which is the Torah."
Rabbi Ḥiyya said, "When the Holy One, blessed be he, revealed Himself [25a] on Mount Sinai to give the Torah to Israel, the earth was appeased and rested satisfied. Thus it is written, *the earth saw and was quiet* (Ps. 140:14)."

We have to make the [following] points:

1. It states, "The Holy One, blessed be he, rejoices in them." Why this lengthy sentence?

2. "For Israel from eight days." How does this prove all that was stated above?

3. Do we need reasons to justify and enumerate the order of separation [between holy and profane]?

4. "Come and see." What is the connection between this matter and the preceding one? Thus, [for instance], "the Holy Land quaked." How is the "Holy Land" connected with the giving of the Torah? It would have been better [to state] "the entire world," for the entire world continues to exist only through the merit of the Torah.[7] Why, then, was the "Holy Land" specified?

5. "Desired to go into the pit." Why was this stated? If the meaning was that it was under the waters of the abyss, why was it phrased so? Let [the passage rather] state, "desired to return to formlessness and void."

6. "The Holy One, blessed be He, said . . . 'O Seat, O Seat!'" He should have stated, "Land, Land"-for the Holy Land was [being addressed]. What does "seat" mean here?

7. Cf. Pesaḥim 68b, Nedarim 32a: "Eleazar b. Shammua said: Were it not for the Torah, heaven and earth would cease to exist."

7. [The passage] states, "He falsifies two covenants," and then enumerates three: Tiferet, Yesod, and Malkhut. Also, how does he falsify these covenants?

8. What is the intention of Rabbi Abba's statement and of his scriptural proof?

Now we will commence explaining this matter with God's help. Rabbi Ḥiyya said, "Worthy are Israel in this world and in the world-to-come." This means that they have a portion in this world, which is Malkhut, and in the world-to-come, which is Binah. This indicates [the greatness of] their level, [reaching up to] Binah.[8] Regarding [the sefirot] which come between Binah and Malkhut, he also stated that "the Holy One, blessed be He, delights in them." He [thus] gave a precondition to [Israel's] coming nigh to holiness, stating that "the Holy One, blessed be He, delights in them." That is similar to our saying, "He has chosen us from among all nations."[9] Previous to this [election], Israel was equal to the other nations. However, "the Holy One, blessed be He, delighted in them" and preferred them and their portion [25b] to the other nations. Thus "they cling [to Him]", referring to Israel's "clinging" to God. This is similar to [the verse], *I am my beloved's, and my beloved is mine* (Song 6:3). For the Holy One, blessed be He, loves Israel, and Israel loves Him.

Since the divine will desires them, and their will and "clinging" are directed toward Him, these [sefirot] constitute the first level of holiness for [Israel]. Afterwards in this manner [Israel] rises to [the level of] Tiferet, for such is the way from the perspective of His having chosen them. They cling to the Shekhinah, which chooses

8. Since Binah was one of the highest sefirot, and consequently relatively removed from human understanding, rising to that level was considered a very significant achievement.

9. This statement is found in the blessing for the Torah in the liturgy.

[them] for its needs and in order to unite herself with her husband, as [Scripture] states, *You shall be My own treasure* (Exod. 19:5). Afterwards, as they cling to her, they are [also] clinging to Tiferet, as [Scripture] states, *You who cleaved to the Lord your God* (Deut. 4:4), referring to Tiferet and 'Ateret.[10]

For this reason [the passage] states, "They . . . are called holy ones," referring to the holy nation [clinging] to Tiferet—"the nation of God," as I have explained. They can thus move themselves [upward] through their occupation with the commandments and [their] clinging [to the divine] until they rise to [the level of the sefirah] Ḥokhmah, which constitutes the place of holiness. This is why [the passage] states, "until He caused them to rise to a high degree which is called 'holy,' as it is written, *Holy is Israel to the Lord*." This is just as we have explained in the Zohar, section Mishpatim. Read it there.[11]

"For Israel." There is a problem here concerning Israel's entering into Malkhut and Yesod so that through "clinging" they might reach Tiferet, as we have explained. The answer [to this difficulty] is that "Israel from eight days." Indeed the mystery of this commandment [of circumcision] is that of entering into Malkhut and Yesod, as is known concerning the recondite meaning of circumcision and the uncovering of the membrane. Thus [the passage] states, "They cling to Him through His Name." The meaning of this is that "Him" is Yesod; "through His Name" signifies Malkhut in the mystery of [the divine name] Shaddai Adonai. Now once they grasp [the meaning of] these names, Shaddai and Adonai, they may afterwards grasp, through the Torah story, the [meaning of the divine] name YHWH. He who does not cling to these two names,

10. 'Ateret is closely connected with Tiferet in the following verses: Isa. 62:3, Jer. 13:18, Prov. 4:9 and 16:31.

11. Zohar II, 108b.

though he may occupy himself with the Torah story, will never attain [meaning of] the name YHWH at all, since he has no [point of] beginning and entry [into this mystery]. Even if he should possess the Torah story, he does not "cling" to it on high. On the contrary, he does harm.

"[The other nations] do not cling to [26a] Him and do not follow His laws." This refers to the establishment of justice and of good qualities, such as mercy, generosity, and silence, which our rabbis, their memory be a blessing, ascribed [to Him] in several places. These are His qualities, may He be blessed, and His laws which are apart from the [laws enumerated in the] Torah. Thus [Scripture] states, *You shall walk in His ways* (Deut. 28:9), *just as He is merciful.*[12]

With this [statement] he indicates the greatness of [Israel's] preparation which the Creator prepared for them and [through which] He chose them. Through this they cling to Malkhut and afterwards, [possessed of] the holy sign [of circumcision], they cling also to Yesod.[13]

All this is an explanation for the earth's quaking. [One might think], "Is Israel holy except through the Torah? If this is so, then anyone accepting the Torah will become holy." Because of this [possible misinterpretation, the passage] said that it is not so. For apart from the Torah, [Israel] has a portion in holiness, in [divine] qualities, and in circumcision. Thus [the passage] stated, "Come and see." The proof of [Israel's] holiness is derived from the fact that the earth quaked. Were this not so, then what complaint could [the earth] have had other than the one we have outlined?

12. Cf. Sotah 14a.

13. Since the sefirah Yesod was a conduit between the "male" Tiferet and the "female" Malkhut, it was connected, by anatomical analogy, with the penis. Hence references to circumcision in Kabbalah were often connected with Yesod.

"He [first] invited the sons of Esau." This has already been explained in the midrash, textually and conceptually. It will be explained in its place, with God's help.

"At that time the Holy Land quaked." It is well known that the Land of Israel and the Torah have a closeness and a relationship similar to that of the life-force to the heart. For the Torah constitutes the life-force of the world, as [the liturgy] states, "He planted eternal life in our midst." The life-force and the soul dwell in the heart and its essential workings are there. Thence it spreads to the rest of the body. The same is true of the Torah. Its essence is in the Land of Israel, and many commandments are dependent upon [the land].[14] There is no doubt that it is more meritorious to perform the commandments in the Land [of Israel] than outside [the Land]. Thus [the performance of] the commandment does not [require] leaving the "dwelling place of the heart." This is the case with the sacrifices.

Thus, knowing this background, when the Land of Israel thought that the Torah would be given to the sons of Esau, the earth quaked and said, "What will come of this is that the Land of Israel will be given to those who [merely] observe the Torah, which is an [earthly] throne directed toward the Land on high." Thus it [will have been] given [26b] to the 'outside' ones, among the *kelipot.* This is why [the passage] stated: "[It] desired to go into the pit of the great abyss." That is to say, it thought that it was abandoning its holiness to [become] the dwelling place of the "outside" ones, whose place is in the "pit of the great abyss." Thus the impure would[15] enter [the Land] to defile the holy. For this

14. Many of the Torah's commandments are only binding upon Jews living in the Land of Israel.

15. The text literally states "would not enter." However, the sense of the passage requires a positive sentence.

reason it was necessary that she leave her place for the "outside." On this account He sat her down [on] "the seats," etc. He said, "Do not think that you are a seat for the 'outside' ones, God forbid. You are [rather] 'seats,' the place of the throne of Glory. Enemies and 'outside' ones will not rule over you, as it is written, *I am the Lord. That is My Name; I will not yield My glory to another* (Isa. 42:8). When you see me take the Torah to Seir and Paran and similar [places], it appears to you that I would be obliged to give the Torah to them so that the world will not be destroyed if Israel does not desire to accept it.[16] This is not so. On the contrary, a thousand worlds will be lost and My Torah will not be given into their hands, God forbid." This is because it would constitute a desecration of the place of Torah, which, as is known, is Tiferet.

"He falsifies two oaths." This has already been explained in the previous passage, for an imperfection in Yesod and Malkhut is the same as one in Tiferet. Therefore it states, "He falsifies two pillars." Now the first imperfection in Tiferet puts it in the category of the "nakedness" of Torah, which we have explained in the previous section. The second [imperfection causes] the two qualities of Yesod and Malkhut to be empty of emanation. That is why it states that "he falsifies the Torah," as I have explained. For the Torah is not worthy of being in force except where Yesod and Malkhut exist.

"He falsifies the pillar of the righteous [Yesod] and the community of Israel," for the Torah was given for this place—of Yesod and Malkhut—and not for another, which is the place of the sons of the handmaid and of the foreskin, as we have explained. In other words, there is an obligation [to give Torah] in this place and not in another. [This signifies] the negation of the "outside" ones. Therefore one who gives [Torah] to the "outside" causes it to leave its proper place and places it among the "outside" ones.

16. Cf. 'Avodah Zarah 3a.

"Rabbi Abba said, 'He falsifies the Torah,'" which is Tiferet, "falsifies the Prophets" [27a], which are Nezaḥ and Hod, "and falsifies the Hagiographa," which are Yesod and Malkhut. This was stated as a proof that just as the Torah is divided into three parts—Torah, Prophets, and Hagiographa—so he who causes the Torah [to dwell] among the "outside" ones does damage to these three [sefirotic] "places." After that, by giving the Torah to the "outside" ones, he certainly [would] cause damage to these three "places."

[Scripture] states, *This is the Torah which Moses placed*, meaning Tiferet. Where was it placed? *Before the children of Israel* (Deut. 4:44), signifying Nezaḥ and Hod. Were the Torah to be given to the "outside" ones, it would be damaged and not be [fit] to be put in the holy place.

"He falsifies the Hagiographa," as it is written, *All your children will be disciples of the Lord* (Isa. 54:13). They are [thus] *disciples of the Lord* and of no one else. That is to say, Nezaḥ and Hod can be termed *disciples of the Lord.* [Thus] when [Scripture] states *all your children*, referring to the children of Israel, [it means that they constitute] a foundation for Tiferet. These and no other are the *disciples of the Lord.* One who replaces them with others certainly causes harm.

[Scripture] further states, *Seal the Torah with My disciples* (Isa. 8:16). This means that only the "disciples" are worthy of the dwelling place of Torah, which is Tiferet. He who replaces them with others causes them harm.

"He falsifies the Hagiographa," as [Scripture] states, *He established a decree in Jacob* (Ps. 78:5). There is no doubt that "Jacob" refers to Malkhut, for there is a difference between "Jacob" and "Israel," as I explained in the book *Pardes* [*Rimmonim*].[17] Since

17. *Pardes Rimmonim*, sec 23, chap. 10, s.v. *ya'akov.* The sefirotic meaning of "Israel" is Tiferet. Cf. Zohar I, 148b.

[Scripture] states *He established a decree in Jacob*," it means that none is worthy of fulfilling the "decree" except for that which is "Jacob." If this is so, then he who brings in "others" causes harm, referring to him who teaches the children of Lilith, the evil maidservant.

Because proof is given here only with reference to Malkhut, [Scripture] also included Yesod in this category when it stated, *Surely the righteous* (Ps. 140:14), which designates the "righteous" [Yesod] and "righteousness" [Malkhut] and refers to their union. *They will instruct* [refers to] one who cuts and circumcises, as I have explained.

It is clear from this passage that one is obliged to shun the Torah instruction of one who is not worthy, particularly with reference to [its] mysteries, as I explained in the previous chapter.

[27b]

PART IV

On the Superiority of This Science to the Other Portions of Our Holy Torah

1

The superiority of this science was related in the Zohar at the end of the ‘Idra[1] in section Naso.[2]

It was taught:
Rabbi Simeon cried, raised his voice, and said:
"Woe." With these words which are revealed here, the comrades of the ‘Idra were hidden away for the world-to-come, and they were removed from this world.
It is proper. . . .

[This] is what we glean from [the passage's] contents:

1. Did Rabbi Simeon bar Yoḥai, peace upon him, believe that the removal of these righteous men constituted a true judgment [in response to] the revelation of the esoteric mystery of the Godhead [at the ‘Idra]? Even if [God] repented of [this judgment], since the intention [of R. Simeon and his colleagues] was for the sake of heaven, nonetheless this testifies to the greatness of the statement in that it was possible that the righteous ones would have been removed for the sin of revelation were it not for the aforementioned reason.

2. That he was informed that their souls had cleaved to higher [worlds] and that they died with a "kiss."[3] This would not have

1. *‘Idra* literally means "threshing floor." It is the title of one of the most significant sections of the Zohar in which esoteric secrets of Torah are revealed. For a full discussion of the significance of the term, see Matt, *Zohar*, p. 278, and Yehuda Liebes, *Perakim be-Millon Sefer ha-Zohar* (Jerusalem, 1982), pp. 93-107.

2. Zohar III, p. 144a.

3. Death by a divine "kiss" was considered the best possible way to die. Baba Batra 17a. Cf. Maimonides, *Guide of the Perplexed* 3.51.

occurred through the study of the other portions of our holy Torah; only from [the study] of this science, which deals with divinity. [This subject] possesses great [power with respect to] cleaving [to higher worlds]. There is no doubt that a man's soul will cleave in the upper world according to his occupations in the lowly world. From [man's] unworthy actions we can learn concerning worthy actions in order to differentiate the superior portion of [divine] service from the remaining portions of service.

[Thus] when a man makes up his mind to turn to the crooked path, it is said of him, *He pays a man according to his actions* (34:11). This means that if one comes to contract impurity, they open the gates [of impurity] for him and make him impure.[4] [It happens] similarly for [one who chooses] the straight path: they lead him according to his path. Thus [one] service [of God] is superior to another, one portion superior to another, just as heaven is higher than the earth. Thus [28a] one who is occupied with divinity will doubtless cling more [to God] than [would have been the case] had he occupied himself with the other portions of the Torah, even though the Torah is entirely divine and consists entirely of His names, may He be blessed.[5]

3. When a man engages in this science, angels and righteous [souls] from the Garden of Eden will accompany him. This is not the case with the other disciplines of Torah. [Rabbi Simeon] taught this when he said, "They did not look upon any place which did not bring forth fragrance."[6] This is a reference to the fragrances and

4. Cf. Shabbat 104a, Yoma 38b.

5. Zohar I, 11a. Cf. Scholem, *On the Kabbalah and Its Symbolism*, pp. 32 ff. Cf. also Moshe Idel, "Tefisat ha-Torah be-Safrut ha-Hekhalot ve-Gilguleha ba-Kabbalah," *Jerusalem Studies in Jewish Thought* 1 (1981): 23-84.

6. This is a continuation of the passage of the 'Idra cited above, n. 2.

perfumes of the Garden of Eden. This matter will be further exposed and revealed in the *Tikkunim* and the other sections of the Zohar. We will explicate it further, with God's help.

4. The pursuit of this science constitutes [the reason for] existence in the world, its life-force and its nourishment. This is what Rabbi Simeon bar Yoḥai, peace upon him, meant [when] he stated: "The world is blessed for their sake." This is clear without a doubt, for pursuing [the study of] divinity causes clinging [to God]. When one clings to the Emanator he will surely be subject to emanation. [Thus] because of this science the world will receive great emanation.

5. [The passage] also teaches the great superiority of those who engage in this science over their colleagues. For in the time of Rabbi Simeon bar Yoḥai, peace upon him, there were a number of tannaim[7] and pious people. Nonetheless [Rabbi Simeon and his colleagues] were superior to the others in their generation by far. [Thus] he said, "We seven are the eyes of God."[8] This refers to their constituting a foundation for the seven higher sefirot. He informed him that Rabbi Simeon was the seventh, who rose above all and influenced all. [Rabbi Simeon's] eminence was also explained in [Zohar] section Bereshit. He was certainly exalted after he had plunged into the pursuit of [this] science and had abandoned almost completely the ways of exoteric learning, though without doubt he devoted a large proportion of his activity to it.

6. [The passage] also teaches the eminence [of Rabbi Simeon and his colleagues]. They were more praiseworthy than the minis-

7. The tannaim were the rabbis of the Mishnah, among whose number R. Simeon b. Yoḥai was counted.

8. This is another continuation of the 'Idra. The "seven" refers to R. Simeon and his colleagues, and contains as well an allusion to the divine power which sustains the earth. Cf. Matt, *Zohar*, pp. 284-285.

tering angels, though they possessed [both] body and soul. Thus [the passage] stated, "We are perplexed." [We learn this] also from Elijah's reply to him. [The passage] also testifies that the ministering angels were gathered at the behest of the Most High to go among them, though this eminence cannot be given a definite value. [28b]

I realize that the reader will question [this exposition] and say, "Have you seen this madman who imagines that the people of our generation can attain this lofty eminence! This is only pride of heart." I would answer him, "Brother, it is not our intention, God forbid, to liken [ourselves] to them [or] even to the hooves of Rabbi Pinḥas' ass.[9] However, we must also consider that the level of exoteric Torah study is not what it was then. Moreover, even if we compare to them from afar, like the light of a darkened star before [the light of] the sun, our pursuit of this science [is still superior] to our pursuit of the exoteric meaning [of Torah]."

Our intention is that one who has pure eyes should also grasp this branch of science and not desist [from his effort]. However, he should [also] not desist, God forbid, from occupying himself with [the study of exoteric] laws, which is work [for the sake of] heaven, as I explained in part I, chapter 6.

9. This is another expression of the notion that contemporary wisdom cannot compare with that of the ancients. The reference to R. Pinḥas' ass is an echo of the Talmudic saying: "If they [the ancients] were as sons of angels, then we are as sons of men, but if they were as the sons of men, then we are as asses, and not like the ass of R. Ḥanina b. Dosa or R. Pinḥas b. Ya'ir but rather like ordinary asses." Shabbat 112b.

2

Having expatiated on the eminence of this science following an exoteric method, we will continue [in the realm of] the esoteric. In the Zohar on the Song of Songs[1] we find:

> *The song of songs, which is Solomon's* (Song 1:11).
> Worthy is the generation in whose midst rests high wisdom.
> The time when the Holy One, blessed be He, desires to reveal on earth that which He has not revealed to the lofty angels.
> What are these [mysteries]?
> The secrets of wisdom of the high engraved name.
> For the holy names were not given to the [angels] but [rather] were given to the sages on earth.
> The [angels] worship and say,
> *O Lord, our God, how great is your Name throughout the earth;*
> *You have covered the heavens with Your splendor* (Ps. 8:2).
> These are the mysteries of the engravings of the holy names which are revealed on earth.
> The praise of [these holy names exists] *upon their heavens.*
> All these [angelic] beings come and praise this fact that He revealed on earth that which He did not reveal to them.

From this [passage], it becomes clear that thc praise which the ministering angels give to the Holy One, blessed be He, does not concern the other portions of the Torah at all, but rather only the mystery of the Name. Moreover, there is no doubt that one who is occupied with the mystery of the Name causes praise of the Holy One, blessed be He, [29a] from the mouths of His angels. This is

1. *Zohar Ḥadash* 61d.

not caused by one who occupies himself with the other portions of the Torah. It was made clear innumerable times in the *Tikkunim* that the eminence of the masters of Kabbalah is much greater [than that] of the masters of Scripture and of Mishnah. It is clear from several sources that the masters of Scripture have an eminence in the mystery of the [World of] "Making,"[2] [that] the masters of Mishnah [have an eminence] in the mystery of the [World of] "Formation,"[3] and [that] the masters of Kabbalah [have an eminence] in the mystery of the [World of] "Creation."[4] This means that the control of the flow of emanation from above to a person [is regulated] according to his occupation in this world. Thus, since the mystery of Scripture inheres in the mystery of the lowest garment of Torah—the stories—[the master of Scripture's] flow of emanation derives solely from the place of "Making." One who occupies himself with Mishnah—that is, the six Orders of Mishnah, consisting of a commentary on the concealed [matters] in the physical Torah and similar matters of [scriptural] exposition—partakes of the mystery of "Formation," as is made clear there. Therefore he derives his flow [of emanation] from the [World] above that of "Making," which is "Formation." The masters of Kabbalah receive more [emanation] from the mystery of the innermost garment, the soul [of Torah] that clothes itself in the commandments, which is the secret of the [World of] "Creation." [Even] the enlightened will be unable to comprehend this matter unless he first examines the book *Pardes [Rimmonim]* in the section Abya.[5] In that place, we have [discussed this matter] at length with God's help.

2. *'Olam ha-'Assiyah*, the lowest of the four sefirotic "worlds," on a par with Scripture, the most elementary form of Judaic learning.

3. *'Olam ha-Yeẓirah*, the next in the hierarchy of "worlds."

4. *'Olam ha-Beriyyah*, the next higher "world." On the nomenclature of these "worlds," cf. Isa. 43:7: "Everyone that is called by My name, for My glory have I created him; I have formed him; I have made him."

5. *Pardes Rimmonim*, sec. 16.

[Kabbalah] also possesses a second advantage [over the rest of Torah] which is [so intimately] connected with the first that they nearly constitute one. This is that the soul (*nefesh*)[6] of one who pursues [the study of] Scripture exclusively stems from [the World of] "Making" and no higher. One who occupies himself with Mishnah rises to the level of [the World of] "Formation," and from [that World] the spirit (*ruaḥ*)[7] descends upon him. The level of one who pursues [the study of] Kabbalah inheres in the mystery of [the World of] "Creation." It is from there that the soul (*neshamah*)[8] comes to him.

There is yet another advantage on top of this. According to the amount of [the master of Kabbalah's] labor he may attain the level of soul [deriving from the World of] Emanation.[9] This is the mystery of the "continuation" which was mentioned above. According to the capacity of [the Kabbalist's] soul is the measure of his "continuation," as is made clear in the book *Pardes [Rimmonim]* in the sections on "soul"[10] and "intention."[11] Study these.

[The master of Kabbalah] also possesses a third advantage which is entwined in the two [29b] preceding ones. That is, one who serves [God] according to the plain meaning [of the Torah] and is drawn after it alone is classified according to the esoteric significance of the term "servants," as it is written, *For it is to Me that the children of Israel are servants; they are My servants* (Lev. 25:55). He who occupies himself with Kabbalah and serves [God] according to the way of Kabbalah in the recondite meaning of the "intention" of the commandments is called "son." Thus [Scripture]

6. The lowest form of the soul.
7. A higher soul-form.
8. The highest form of the soul.
9. The highest of the four sefirotic "worlds."
10. Cordovero, *Pardes Rimmonim*, sec. 31.
11. Ibid., sec. 32. "Intention" refers to the consciousness that the action one is about to undertake is done for the sake of fulfilling a divine commandment.

states, *You are sons to the Lord your God* (Deut. 14:1). There are many similar [verses], such as *My firstborn son is Israel* (Exod. 4:22). These praises are elaborated upon in the *Tikkunim*, the *Ra'aya Mehemna*, and countless times in the *pikkudin*.

[The Kabbalist] has yet a fourth advantage, for one who pursues the plain meaning [of the Torah] is liable to err in the intention of his prayer, thinking that God, may He be blessed, is capable of change, will, love, and similar things. Thus when he says [in prayer], "You chose us from among all the nations, You loved us and desired us," the poor fellow thinks that God relates to him through love. From this it follows that He could also relate to him through hatred, as [Scripture] states, *I loved you, said the Lord . . . and I hated Esau* (Mal. 1:2-3). He would also be led [to believe in] many changes [in God]. This [notion with regard] to the First Existent certainly constitutes a false belief. Would that this person not add [further] transgression to his sin. [On the other hand,] he who pursues [the study of] Kabbalah knows the nature of the sefirot and regulates his divine service through them and the high providence. He will adjust his intentions as is proper. Only one who has arrived at [this knowledge] will attain this advantage.

[Kabbalah] enjoys also a fifth advantage. One who prays like a day-old baby (in accordance with the opinion of some latter-day [authorities] who have dismissed the pursuit of this science and whom I will not name) will doubtless not receive except [that which pertains] to a day-old baby. Thus a baby does not understand the need for clothing or for acquiring that which is necessary for true happiness. All his effort is given to unnecessary matters, from which one derives neither wholeness nor its opposite, such as cravings and merriment and "running to the sound of the drum"[12]—

12. Mo'ed Katan 9b.

i.e., material things. [However,] he who concentrates his mind [in prayer] like an elder will be answered according to his understanding. He will receive according to [30a] the attainment of his understanding. If in his requests [in prayer], he concentrated on the benefit of the Shekhinah, without a doubt all the emanation [reaching him] will be there in the lofty light. Between these [two worshippers] there exists a difference [so great] that the mind cannot grasp it. This matter will become clear to the reader after he delves a bit into this science, with God's help.

There is yet a sixth advantage. A number of sections, commandments, and interpretations of our holy Torah are astounding to the reader and difficult to properly comprehend. However, when the reader becomes accustomed to this science, all these matters will be clarified for him beyond any doubt. Gates which were shut in the face of ordinary investigation will be opened. He will also find it easier [to comprehend] some interpretations of our holy Torah, as is known from the sayings of our rabbis, their memory be a blessing, without a doubt.

[The Kabbalist] also possesses a great advantage more valuable than all [the others] and which persists in the world of souls, as is explained in the Zohar, section Ḥayyei Sarah.[13]

> Worthy are those righteous for whom much good is stored away for that [future] world.
> [In that world] the innermost place of all of these is [reserved] for those who know the secret of their Master and know to cling to Him daily.
> Of these it is written:
> *No eye has seen [them], O God, but You, who act for those who trust in Him* (Isa. 64:3).

13. Zohar I, 130b.

As Scripture says:
[Elihu] waited out Job's speech (Job 32:4).
This [refers to] the ones who urge themselves [to understand] the word of wisdom and [examine it] fastidiously.
They wait upon it to understand the truth of the word and to know their Master.
These are the ones whom their Master praises every day.
These are the ones who come among the lofty holy ones.
They enter into all the lofty gates.
There is no one who will prevent them.
Happy is their portion in this world and in the world that is coming.

From this [passage] there is another proof that the essence of [Scripture's] statement *Know the God of your father* (I Chron. 28:9) refers to the pursuit of this science. [Thus the passage] stated, "to know their Master." It also appears that one must pursue the knowledge of hidden things with great punctiliousness, concentration, and analysis. This is the opposite [of the opinion] of would-be Kabbalists in our generation who say that one need not be exact in this science.

[30b]

PART V

On the Virtues of This Science Beyond [Those of] the Other Portions of Our Holy Torah

1

The first virtue [of Kabbalah] is that when a man occupies himself with [divine] attributes[1] his words have ramifications on high and the sefirot arrange themselves in accordance with the matter he is pursuing. [This is] conditional on the requisite purity and knowledge [residing in] him. Thus have they explained in the Zohar, section Naso in the 'Idra, when Rabbi Simeon and his colleagues completed all the adornments of the Ancient of Days.[2] There it states:[3]

> Rabbi Simeon said to the colleagues:
> "When we will arrange this canopy, which you see upon us, I see that all the adornments have fallen in its midst and they shed light in this place."
> One curtain of the holy light was spread on four pillars in the four directions.
> One pillar stood from below to above, and there was one shovel in its hand.
> And in the shovel there were four diverse openings [situated] on all its sides.
> They grasped the curtain and brought it down from above to below.
> The same for the second pillar and the third and the fourth.
> Between each pillar there were attached eighteen legs of the pillars which were lighted with the candle which was engraved upon that covering.

1. A reference to the sefirot.
2. A reference to the sefirah Keter in its connection with Eyn Sof.
3. Zohar III,134b.

Similarly for the four sides.
We see these adornments shed light on it, for the words from our mouths were waiting to be crowned and to arise each one to its place.
When [the word] was adorned in our mouths, each one left and was crowned and adorned in that adornment which had been adorned here from all our mouths.
At the time when all of us opened our mouths to adorn in that adornment, that adornment would sit and wait for the word which will come out of your mouths.
Then it leaves [31a] for its place to be crowned and is crowned.
All the angelic supporters [of the heavenly throne] from this side and from that side rejoiced, since they had heard that which they did not know and they listened to your voices.
How many [angelic] chariots were present here on your account.
Worthy are you for the world that is coming.
For all these words which emerge from your mouths are holy words, all proper words which do not diverge to the right or left.
The Holy one, blessed be He, rejoiced to hear and discern these words until He completed the judgment that in the world that is coming you will say another time all these holy words.
Of you it is written:
Your mouth is like choicest wine. Let it flow to my beloved as new wine gliding over the lips of sleepers (Song of Songs 7:10).
Even in the world that is coming his lips will move before him.

From this [passage] the eminence and virtue of [this] science is established. For just as a man brings forth words from his mouth and arranges them, so the sefirot are arranged on high. Accompanying this is another virtue: that he will occupy himself with that matter in the world-to-come. This is the secret meaning of the saying of [the sages], may their memory be blessed, "His lips move in the grave."[4] It seems, indeed, that this refers especially to this science. Rabbi Simeon bar Yoḥai, peace upon him, explained this in another place.

The reason for this matter is that when a man's soul leaves [him], without doubt it will attach itself to the place which it enlightened when it was living its life. Therefore the mystery of awakening is the aforementioned illumination, when the soul leaves to receive its reward. This is called, in bodily terms, moving [lips] in the grave. Similarly the soul [enjoys] this eminence on high. Even if we admit that this may also occur [regarding Torah interpreted] according to its plain meaning, there is no doubt that with regard to Kabbalah the [illumination] rises to a sublime level.

[Kabbalah] also possesses a third virtue. It is that the one who pursues this science will know how to unify his Master and to serve him with a complete heart. Thus Rabbi Simeon bar Yoḥai, peace upon him, explained in [the Zohar], section Be-shalaḥ.[5]

> *The Lord is near to all who call Him, to all who call Him with sincerity* (Ps. 145:18).
> What does *with sincerity* mean?
> It is as they have explained:
> —That he know to unify the Holy Name as is proper.
> This is the service of the Holy Name.
> One who knows to unify the Holy Name [31b] sustains [the nation which is] unique in the world, as it is written:
> *And who is like Your nation Israel, a unique nation on earth?* (II Sam. 7:23).
> Therefore they interpreted:
> Any priest who does not know how to unify the Holy Name as is proper, his service is no service.

4. Yevamot 97a. Cf. Yerushalmi, Shekalim 2a; Pesikta Rabbati 2:5.
5. Zohar II, 57a.

For all depends upon him, both the upper service and the lower service.
He needs to concentrate his heart and his will in order that upper and lower beings alike be blessed.
It is written:
When you come to see My face (Isa. 1:12).
Each son of man who comes to unify the Holy Name and does not concentrate his heart and will with awe in order that [both] upper and lower [beings] be blessed through him, they throw his prayer outside, and all announce evil of him.
The Holy One, blessed be He, says concerning Him:
When you come to see my face.
[The verse] should have stated, *to see My face.*
What does *to see* [signify]?
Rather all those faces of the King are hidden in the depths beyond the darkness.
All those who know how to unify the Holy Name properly split all those walls of darkness, and the face of the King are seen and illuminated.
All are blessed—upper and lower [beings].
Similarly blessings are found in all the worlds.
Thus it is written:

When you come to see My face . . . who asked this of you?
What does [the verse] come to teach?
That he who comes to unify the lofty Name needs to unify from this crown, as it is written:
With this shall Aaron come to the holy place (Lev. 16:3)—in order that these two, the righteous [Yesod] and righteousness [Malkhut] should unite as one.
In this union [is found] blessing in order that all should unite upon them.
These are called [as in] that which is written:
Happy is the man You choose and bring near to dwell in Your courts (Ps. 65:5).

If he comes to unify the Holy Name and does not concentrate his heart and will on [the unification] with awe, the Holy One, blessed be He, says:
Who has asked this of you—to trample My courts?
Certainly blessings will not be found among them.
On the contrary, judgment inheres in them, which is found in all.

From [this passage] it appears that the service of one who does not know how to unify [the Holy Name] is no service. From this it is also clear that the prayer of one who does not know how to unify properly is unfit. One will not discover this matter except [32a] through the deep pursuit of this science, with God's help.

[Kabbalah] has also a fourth virtue. It is that a man possesses a portion [of the Worlds of] Making, Formation, Creation, and Emanation. All is according to the merit of his deeds, as we have explained in the book *Pardes [Rimmonim]* in the section on "Soul." Now the portion [of the World of] Making is clothed in the mystery of the performance of the physical commandments. The portion [of the World of] Formation [is clothed] in the mystery of the intention of the commandments according to their plain meaning. From the [World of] Creation and higher, [the portions] will only be clothed in the mystery of Kabbalah and in [the person's] concentration on it, as we have explained in the aforementioned [section of the] *Pardes [Rimmonim].* Without a doubt he who has not pursued this science will be unable to complete the aforementioned portion in any other way, [even] if he is worthy of it.

2

The fifth virtue [of Kabbalah] is that one who pursues this science will know how to explain several matters in the Torah which are difficult for those who rely upon the plain meaning [of Scripture], such as superfluous letters, ones which are written but not pronounced or pronounced and not written, and similar [cases].[1] For example, in the verse *You will bring them and plant them* (Exod. 15:17), there is a superfluous *vav.* Similarly [in the verse] *You will bring upon them fear and dread* (Exod. 15:16). The word "fear" [*'ematah*] should have been written without the superfluous *tav.* In the Zohar, section Be-shalaḥ, it was explained in this way:[2]

> *You will bring upon them fear ('ematah) and dread.*
> The verse should have read *fear* (*'emah*).
> What is the significance of *'ematah*?
> For you have no word or letter in the Torah which does not contain lofty mysteries.
> Said Rabbi Simeon:
> It is as if [it referred to] the fear of the Shekhinah.
> In the same manner [we interpret] *you will bring them* (*teviamo*).
> [Scripture] should have used [the form] *teviam.*
> What does *teviamo* signify?
> The Holy Spirit said concerning the last generation which Joshua circumcised,[3] among whom was revealed the revelation

1. The Biblical text, as preserved by the Masoretes, contains numerous cases where a grammatical analysis required that the text be modified. Since the text itself was sacrosanct, the purpose was achieved in these ways.

2. Zohar II, 59b.

3. Cf. Josh. 5:2-9.

of the holy sign of the Name of the Holy One, blessed be He.
For those clung to Him through the letter *vav*[4] and are worthy to inherit the land, as it is said:
When your nation are all righteous, they will inherit the land forever (Isa. 60:21).
All those whom [Joshua] circumcised, to whom was revealed the holy sign, and those who guard [it] are called righteous.
For that reason, *they will inherit the land forever.*
Therefore, *teviamo* contains a superfluous *vav.*
Teviamo is [spelled] plene. [32b]
[Thus] you have no word or [even] the smallest letter in the Torah which does not contain in itself lofty mysteries and holy wisdom.
Happy is the portion of those who know it.

If one should ask this question of a grammarian, he would answer that [the preceding examples] are among the letters which are [seemingly] superfluous. In our opinion, one who says that there is a superfluous [*yeter*] letter in the Torah should have his teeth taken out [*yutru*] if [he says it] deliberately. If [he says it] in error, then his Master will forgive him.

The sixth virtue [of Kabbalah]: There are words in the Torah which are improper and ungrammatical according to [their] simple meaning. Thus the Torah states, *Inscribe this in a document as a reminder, and read it aloud to Joshua* (Exod. 17:14). By the [Temple] service! One of those who aspired to [divine] service asked me, "What does it mean, *and read it aloud to Joshua*? [Scripture] should have stated, 'speak to Joshua.' For *and read it aloud* [seems to] indicate that he [actually] wrote the section and placed it, God forbid, into his ears." I replied to him in a plain manner that the Torah speaks in the language of the sons of men, for thus would a

4. The letter *vav* symbolized the sefirah Yesod, which Kabbalists connected with circumcision. Cf. Elliot Wolfson, "Letter Symbolism and Anthropomorphic Imagery in the Zohar," *Jerusalem Studies in Jewish Thought* 8 (1989): 172.

man speak to his fellow concerning the strengthening of the [divine] command. He replied, "I will not believe that there is not something here that is not known to us, through which the wording would become proper." I said [of him] to one who knows the science [of Kabbalah], "To [men like] these I apply [the verse] *[Behold,] the tears of the oppressed, and they have no comforter* (Eccles. 4:1)," [referring] to those for whom the words of Torah are oppressed and stolen from their minds. [Then] I explained the matter in the way of truth, as will become clear in its place, with God's help.

The seventh virtue [of Kabbalah] is that he who pursues this science and fills his mouth with joy because of it, will without doubt fill his heart with fear of heaven and fear of sin, and will redouble his efforts in [divine] service. This is indubitable. For even the reading of the words of the Zohar will bring a man joy of the soul in the fear of God, as if he pursued [his studies] with the righteous in the Garden of Eden. And if the person himself does not see [it], his "constellation"[5] does, for there is no doubt that this is the essential pursuit of the Torah among the righteous in the Garden of Eden.

The eighth virtue [of Kabbalah] concerns that which I myself have experienced, especially in the matter of "exiles."[6] For we would "exile" ourselves to the field with the divine Rabbi [33a] Solomon ben Alkabetz[7] the Levite, may God preserve him, to occupy ourselves with the verses of the Torah extemporaneously without study in depth. [Then] many times matters were innovated which no one could understand unless he saw or experienced the

5. Cf. Megillah 3a, Sanhedrin 94a.

6. Cordovero wrote a book containing the Kabbalistic interpretations which were revealed to him during these "exiles." It was published as *Sefer Gerushin* (Venice, ca. 1602).

7. Solomon ha-Levi Alkabetz (ca. 1505-1584) was Cordovero's brother-in-law and his teacher in Kabbalah.

matter. The gifts which I received in the "exiles" and which came into my portion through God's grace to me I will write down in a separate composition, dividing them into chapters one by one with God's help.

The ninth virtue [of Kabbalah] is something I have also seen through experience. If one concentrates in prayer according to the way of truth, the matter [he is praying for] will be accomplished of itself. The "outside" ones have no power to interrupt it through vain thoughts, as will happen to a man who concentrates [in prayer] according to the way of the simple meaning. The reason for this is that the simple meaning is in the place where the *kelipot* can reach. Thus the "outside" one's accusations can hold sway there. However [if one prays] according to the way of Kabbalah, [the "outside" one] has no sway at all there.

The tenth virtue [of Kabbalah] is something that I have tested and experienced. [It is] that he who has not entered into the holy covenant will never master this science.[8] Even if they speak of and discourse upon the sefirot, they do not know and do not understand. They walk in darkness. They have no power to understand at all, even the simple things. This is not the case with the simple meaning, for there are already some of them who can study Halakhah according to its simple meaning. This is doubtless because of the reason I have mentioned.

Added to these virtues are several other advantages, as the reader will see for himself with God's help. However, we have [only] mentioned a few of them in order to influence the reader [to pursue] the science to the greatest extent possible. [For these omissions] we ask God's forgiveness and absolution.

8. This refers to the phenomenon of Christian Hebraists encountering the Kabbalah and appropriating it for Christian theological purposes. Cf. Joseph L. Blau, *The Christian Interpretation of the Cabala in the Renaissance* (New York, 1944). Cf. also Elliot Wolfson, "Circumcision and the Divine Name," pp. 103-106.

[33b]

PART VI

On the Necessary Preparation for Beginners in This Science [Arranged According to the] Sections of the Book *Pardes* [*Rimmonim*]

1

[Sec. 1] First of all, [the beginner] must know that the Creator, Eyn Sof, is one and has no second. He is the Cause of Causes and the Prime Mover. He is not one in the numerical sense, for [the concepts of] mutation and change and form and multiplicity do not apply to Him. [One] is rather a word utilized by way of parable and likeness, since the number one stands by itself and is the beginning of each number, all numbers [being contained] within it in potential, while it is a part of every number in actuality.

When they call the Creator, may He be blessed, One, it is in this manner: that the Creator, may He be blessed, [is found] in all things in actuality, while all things are [found] in Him in potential. He is the beginning and cause of all things. In this way they ascribed to the Creator, may He be blessed, unity, without change by addition or subtraction, similar to the [number] one. [They found] also that He is the [necessary] Cause of being, just as [the number] one is necessary for [all] numbers, for no number could be in existence without it. He is not a number. If the one should be eliminated, [all] numbers would be eliminated, [whereas] if the numbers should be eliminated, the one would not be eliminated in their elimination. This is the power of [the divine] unity.

This is the case with the Creator, may He be blessed. He is the agent and the creator of all, and sustains being. Should the action [of the agent] be eliminated, the agent would not be eliminated, since He has no need of any of them. Should being be eliminated, He would not be eliminated in its elimination, since He has no need of being and exists by Himself. All those who pursue the divine science agree to this.

2. [The beginner] needs to know that Eyn Sof caused and emanated His sefirot, and His actions are [performed] through them. They constitute the ten "sayings" through which he acts.[1] They serve him as vessels for the [34a] actions which derive from Him in the World of Separation[2] and below. Truly His being and essence extend themselves in them, as we will explain in greater detail.

[Sec. 2] These sefirot are ten and not nine; ten and not eleven. One cannot add to them, nor can one subtract from them, for thus His wisdom decreed, may He be blessed. He knows that [for] the purpose intended in their emanation it was necessary [to attain] this complete number, for we have not attained [knowledge of] a lesser or greater [number] at all.

This [number] is not to be connected to the [divine] "qualities" alone, but rather [also] to the things which derive from them. All of them are included in the ten. The "qualities" themselves have as their sum ten from ten. One may not add or subtract, God forbid. Even if we were to say that [the ten] are the sum of the six directions and the four qualities,[3] and so on, the intention is that they reveal themselves in the mystery of four, and the like. However, their sum is always ten. The true and apparent reason for this was explained by King David, peace upon him, when he said, *You, O Lord my God, have done many things; the wonders You have devised for us* (Ps. 40:6). [In the Mishnah] it is taught, "There are three crowns."[4] It is known that the crowns are reserved for the president [of the Sanhedrin], the high priest, and the king. Because

1. Cf. Mishnah, Avot 5:1: "The world was created by ten [divine] statements."

2. That is, the world which does not partake in the complete divine Unity.

3. Cf. *Sefer Yeẓirah* 1:5.

4. Mishnah, Avot 4:17.

of the awesomeness of their majesty, it was necessary to have, [respectively,] a deputy [high priest], a viceroy, and a vice-president[5] of the court for the administration of the nation. Under these [officials] are three flocks of sheep: the hosts of Israel, the watches of the priesthood, the officers who direct the people and the Sanhedrin. All of them have their eyes and their hearts on "the crown of a good name"[6] [from] the congregation of Jacob,[7] which rises upward with their help to glorify their Maker for His creation, *for that is the entire [duty of] man* (Eccles. 12:13). Behold, I have shown [in front of] your very eyes the need for this complete number, *which tells its end from [its] beginning* (cf. Isa. 46:10).

3. [The beginner] needs to know that these [divine] qualities possess [holy] names which may not be erased.[8] They [along with their sefirotic equivalents] are: Ehyeh = Keter; Yah = Ḥokhmah; YHWH (with the punctuation of the name 'Elohim) = Binah; 'El = Ḥesed; 'Elohim = Gevurah; YHWH = Tiferet; Ẓeva'ot = Neẓaḥ; Shaddai or El Ḥai = Yesod; Adonai = Malkhut. These names are [34b] the sefirot. It is not that these names are ascribed to the sefirot, God forbid. On the contrary, the [divine] names [themselves] are the sefirot, and the names are appellations of Eyn Sof according to His actions. [Thus] everywhere that the name of [divine] *being* (*havayah*) is described, as we will mention below, these ten names will reveal the specifics of *being* and its rules. Thus the end of the [letter] *yod*, which hints at the upper "Crown" (*keter*), which name is not pronounced, is called by the name Ehyeh. The *yod* itself, in any place, has as its particular name Yah.

5. *Av bet din*, lit. "father of the court."
6. Mishnah, Avot 4:17.
7. A reference to the sefirah Malkhut.
8. This is because of the intrinsic holiness of these names.

This [is the case] for all of them. Thus we have a wondrous unity. The praise and thanksgiving and prayer and unification that we make [utilizing] these names [which may be] pronounced, might be considered by the listener as concerning only one sefirah or two, God forbid, in accordance with the [divine] names and the details. However, it consists, rather, of a unification of all ten sefirot and the ten "beings" which we will mention in chapter 5.[9] Then these things will be revealed in our mouths and in our hearts [regarding] that singular Divine Name which is used for that specific organ which is included in all the ten "beings." Thus the general has need of the specific, and the specific has need of the general[10] in the power of the true, wondrous Unity.

[Sec. 3] 4. [The beginner] must know that Eyn Sof is not [identical with] Keter, as many have thought. Eyn Sof is, rather, the cause of Keter, and Keter is derived from Eyn Sof, which is the Cause of Causes. He must also know that Eyn Sof is the First Cause of all that exists, for there is no cause above it. Keter is the first derivative of it. From Keter goes forth the process of the rest of emanation. This does not contradict [the fact] that Keter is counted among the sefirot, as many have thought. It is counted among the ten and is considered in importance [similar to] the emanated [sefirot] themselves. Indeed, from the standpoint of the generality of the ten emanated [sefirot], Keter is not revealed among them due to its loftiness. However, [in that case] they [maintain the "tenness" of the sefirot by] including Da'at in place of Keter.[11]

9. Cf. pt. VI, chap. 5 below.

10. This is one of the thirteen exegetical principles of R. Ishmael, found at the beginning of Sifra, a Tannaitic midrash. The "general" and "specific" refer to general principles being illustrated by concrete scriptural verses, and vice versa.

11. On the complementary sefirah, Da'at, see Scholem, *Kabbalah*, pp. 107 ff.

5. [The beginner] needs to know that the aforementioned Da'at is not itself a sefirah, God forbid. It is, rather, an aspect of the six "directions" [35a] which are centered above among the first sefirot. It is the mystery of the *vav* which is hidden in Keter, Ḥokhmah, and Binah, as will be explained. It is the essence of the sefirot emanated below[12] and not a sefirah itself, as many have thought.

[Sec. 4] 6. [The beginner] must know that regarding Eyn Sof, King of the King of Kings, it is inappropriate for us to say of Him "blessed" or "magnified" or "praised" or the like, since He cannot be blessed by another or praised or magnified. Rather is He the Blesser, Praiser, Magnifier, and Giver of Life from the very beginning of His emanation to [its] farthest point, "from the horns of buffaloes to the eggs of lice."[13] Before the formation of the universe [Eyn Sof] had no need of emanation, as is known. He was concealed in His holy and pure simplicity. It is inappropriate [to posit] of Him any letter or vowel or image, for even Keter, which is the beginning of emanation, has no name or image in letter or vowel. How much more so [is this the case] with the King of the King of Kings, whom we cannot imagine and of whom we cannot speak or posit either judgment or mercy, passion or anger, change or boundedness, sleep or motion, or any quality whatsoever, either prior to the emanation or now after the emanation.

What we can indeed know is that at the commencement of all, Eyn Sof emanated the fine emanation which [consists of] the ten sefirot which are forms of thought and are from His essence and cling to Him. He and they are all [included] in a complete unity. These [ten "fine"] sefirot are souls which garb themselves in the ten

12. The numerical equivalent of the Hebrew letter *vav* is six. This symbolizes the six sefirot emanated after Keter, Ḥokhmah, and Binah, which were present in essence in the higher sefirot.

13. Cf. Shabbat 107b.

sefirot which are called by name and which are as vessels for the aforementioned entities. They are [the locus of] judgment and mercy and the aforementioned activities which we must not ascribe to Eyn Sof. And [we must not even ascribe these activities] to [the sefirot] in actuality but rather [to them] as they garb themselves in [the "worlds" of] "Creation," "Formation," and "Making," as we will explain further, with God's help.[14]

[Sec. 5] 7. [The beginner] must also know that before [35b] the emanation of the aforementioned qualities, these qualities were utterly hidden within Him in the greatest possible unity. It is not appropriate [to ascribe to them] any image or point at all. They were, rather, united in Him. Afterward He emanated one point from Himself. [This] one emanation is Keter, which is called 'Ayin ("Nothingness") on account of its great transparency and closeness to its source, such that being (*yesh*) cannot be posited of it. From [Keter] a second point was emanated in a second revelation. It is Ḥokhmah, and it is called "being" because it is the beginning of revelation and being. It is called "being from nothingness" (*yesh me-'ayin*). Because it is the beginning of being and not being itself, it required a third point for the revelation of existents. That is [the sefirah] Binah, which [constitutes] the revelation of the existents. Ḥokhmah is the beginning of existence, and Binah is the end of existence, since the beginning of the founding of existence comes from Ḥokhmah, which is called "Beginning" (*re'shit*).[15] The end of their concealment is in the supernal Jubilee,[16] as is known.

From these three [sefirot] came forth the six "directions" of [Divine] Providence, which consist [of the sefirot] from Ḥesed and

14. See above, pt. IV, chap. 2, nn. 2-4.

15. Cf. Ps. 111:10: "The beginning of wisdom (*re'shit ḥokhmah*) is the fear of God."

16. A reference to the sefirah Binah.

below. First of all Ḥesed [derived from] Ḥokhmah. After that Gevurah emanated from Binah. After that Tiferet emanated from Keter. The revelation of all three came about through Binah except that the essence of their roots [came from] Ḥokhmah and Keter respectively. Now within these three, Neẓaḥ, Hod, and Yesod were hidden. After the emanation and revelation of the three aforementioned [sefirot], Neẓaḥ was revealed from Ḥesed, Hod was revealed from Gevurah, and Yesod from Tiferet. Now the emanation of Malkhut indeed [took place] along [with that] of the six "directions." [However,] it will be explained in another place with God's help.

Accordingly, the order of emanation [occurred] in one of three ways, all of which are true: either one after the other, Keter, Ḥokhmah, Binah, Gedulah . . . to Malkhut; or else Keter, Tiferet, Yesod, and Malkhut constitute one point, which propagated itself to the end of Malkhut, while Ḥokhmah, Ḥesed, and Neẓaḥ constitute a second point, which propagated itself until Neẓaḥ and Binah, Gevurah and Hod are a third point, which propagates itself until Hod. Alternatively, Keter, Ḥokhmah, Binah. Afterwards, Ḥesed, Gevurah, Tiferet. Afterwards, Neẓaḥ. Hod, Yesod. Malkhut [36a] is the sum of all. With this, this chapter is summed up, with God's help.

2

[Sec. 6] 8. [The beginner] must also know that the most popular and agreed-upon way among Kabbalists to describe the sefirot is the following: Keter, Ḥokhmah, and Binah [forming] the likeness of a triangle.[1] Under them, Gedulah, Gevurah, and Tiferet [forming] the likeness of a triangle. Also, Neẓaḥ, Hod, and Yesod [forming] a second triangle. Malkhut is centered under them.

Now the reason for this [depiction] is that Keter is the reason and cause for [the existence] of Ḥokhmah and Binah together. Therefore it is depicted above them. As well, Binah has a second cause, namely Ḥokhmah. Thus Ḥokhmah precedes Binah. Binah is therefore lower than both of them. Now Ḥokhmah is the root of Ḥesed, Keter is the root of Mercy,[2] and Binah is the root of Judgment.[3] This way is to be followed for them all.

9. [The beginner] must also know that Keter [is found] in Ḥokhmah, Ḥokhmah in Binah, Binah in Ḥesed, Ḥesed in Gevurah, Gevurah in Tiferet, Tiferet in Neẓaḥ, Neẓaḥ in Hod, Hod in Yesod, and Yesod in Malkhut. Similarly, Malkhut [is found] in Yesod, Yesod in Hod, Hod in Neẓaḥ, Neẓaḥ in Tiferet, Tiferet in Gevurah, Gevurah in Ḥesed, Ḥesed in Binah, Binah in Ḥokhmah, and Ḥokhmah in Keter. The reason is that the upper [sefirot] need the lower ones, and the lower ones need the upper ones. Thus the

1. Literally a *segol,* the triangular-shaped Hebrew vowel. In this case, the *segol* is an inverted one with one dot on top and two on the bottom. The upper point would refer to Keter, and the other two to Ḥokhmah and Binah respectively.

2. Within Keter, the highest of the sefirot, it was assumed that, with judgment yet undifferentiated, nothing but mercy prevailed.

3. Binah was considered to be the sefirotic source of judgment and evil.

strength of the lower [sefirot] is in the upper ones, and the strength of the upper [sefirot] is in the lower ones. All of them need Eyn Sof, while He has need of none of them.

10. [The beginner] must also know that these sefirot have no [physical] location, God forbid, though we ascribe form to them in order [to render them] intelligible. However, the truth is that Eyn Sof is the locus for its [ten emanated] sefirot, and Keter is the locus of nine sefirot, and Ḥokhmah is the locus of eight [sefirot], and Binah is the locus of seven [sefirot], and so on for them all. Malkhut is the locus for the [World of] Creation; the [World of] Creation is the locus for the [world of] Formation], [and] the [World of] Formation is the locus of [the World of] Making[4] until the [emanation] reaches the earth, which is enclosed in the sphere of the element of water. The element [36b] of water is inside the sphere of the element of air, and the element of air is inside the sphere of the element of fire. These four elements are inside the spheres, with each product surrounded by its cause until the finish of the degrees.[5]

[Sec. 7] 11. [The beginner] must also know that [the Kabbalists] have ascribed "channels" to the sefirot. The reason for this [is that God] has arranged a line of "illumination" from the first sefirah to its counterpart, and has arranged a line of "illumination" from the counterpart [sefirah] to the influencing [sefirah] in order to receive from it. Now the coming together of these two aspects of light is called "channels." Indeed there are innumerable channels of various types. Among them are these: one from Keter to Ḥokhmah, and one from Keter to Binah, and one from Keter to Tiferet, totaling three; one from Ḥokhmah to Binah, one from Ḥokhmah from Ḥesed, one from Ḥokhmah to Gevurah, and one from

4. On these "worlds," see Scholem, *Kabbalah*, pp. 118-119.
5. Cf. Maimonides, *Mishneh Torah*, Hilkhot Yesodei ha-Torah 4:1-5.

Ḥokhmah to Tiferet, totaling four; one from Binah to Ḥesed, one from Binah to Gevurah, and one from Binah to Tiferet, totaling three; one from Ḥesed to Neẓaḥ, one from Ḥesed to Gevurah, and one from Ḥesed to Tiferet, totaling three; one from Gevurah to Hod [and] one from Gevurah to Tiferet, totalling two; one from Tiferet to Neẓaḥ, one from Tiferet to Hod, and one from Tiferet to Yesod, totaling three; one from Neẓaḥ to Hod [and] one from Neẓaḥ to Yesod, totaling two; one from Hod to Yesod, and one from Yesod to Malkhut. Malkhut receives nothing except from Yesod alone. Through it, it receives from all [the sefirot]. Without [Yesod, Malkhut] cannot receive [emanation] from any of them, and no one of the [sefirotic] qualities is able to influence the lower [worlds] without it, for it is essential for the guidance of the lower [worlds]. These are the major channels. In addition to them there can be an infinity of [sefirotic] combinations.

[Sec. 8] 12. [The beginner] must also know that the sefirot have the power to perform opposite actions, at times [partaking of] Judgment, and at times [partaking] of Mercy. All of the [sefirot] always agree on the [various] actions, for none of them will perform an action except through them all and with all of them in agreement through [the agency of] Malkhut.

To introduce the matter, each of the [sefirot] is made up of [all] ten. Moreover, [37a] they [individually] possess revealed principles. At times [these are] three: Ḥesed, Din, and Raḥamim,[6] and sometimes four, including the aforementioned three and one made up of them all. This is the mystery of the element of earth, which is made up of three elements: fire, water, and air. Sometimes it is made up of five which constitute a mystery: Ḥesed, Gevurah, Tiferet, Neẓaḥ, [and] Hod. Sometimes [it is made up of] six which

6. Lovingkindness, judgment, and mercy.

constitute the six "directions,"[7] and sometimes of seven which constitute [the sefirot] from Ḥesed to Malkhut. Sometimes [it is made up of] eight, including Binah, and sometimes of ten from Keter on down or from Ḥokhmah and below, with Da'at completing the number, as we have [previously] explained. This notion of combination does not imply mere combination among them, for never do [the sefirot] have less than ten. However, the intention is that all of them combine in three or four [combinations], and they appear in that guise in illumination and revelation.

13. [The beginner] must also know the idea with regard to Keter—that the ancients explained that it possesses 620 columns of light. There is no doubt that these 620 develop one from another as a result [develops] from a cause, while all of them are [contained] within the first effect. This [sefirotic] quality consists [entirely of] Mercy; Judgment does not rule there at all. Thus Ḥokhmah is also Mercy, as is Binah. However, though Binah consists of Mercy, judgments arise from it, as the Zohar explains.[8] [Thus] its essence is mercy, [though] from it is the awakening of Judgment, which is the mysterious working of the root of Gevurah that is in her. It [thus] contains within itself the roots of Mercy and Ḥesed, as is known.

14. [The beginner] must also know that the origin of Judgment[9] is on high in the will of the Emanator. However, it is hidden, as all of the qualities were hidden in Keter and Eyn Sof and were united there. There none of the qualities were revealed. Thus the action of Judgment was hidden in the first three [sefirot], while it did not appear there until its place of revelation in Gevurah.

15. [The beginner] must also know that the connection between the sefirot and their union, despite the fact that one [repre-

7. The six lower sefirot from Gedulah to Yesod.

8. Cf. Zohar I, 151a, 220b; III, 10b, 15b, 99a, 118b, 262a.

9. I.e., evil. It was inconceivable to assign evil an independent existence.

sents] Judgment and another Mercy, is by virtue of [the fact that] Ḥesed includes Gevurah and the other qualities. Thus Gevurah is intertwined with Ḥesed [37b] in one of two ways. Firstly through [the essence of] Gevurah which is in Ḥesed, which means that [the quality of] Gevurah [in Ḥesed is attracted to] Gevurah. Through this [attraction] they agree upon one action. The second way is that of [the essence of] Ḥesed in Gevurah, for Ḥesed [in Gevurah] is intertwined with [the sefirah] Ḥesed, and thus they agree upon one action. Thus Tiferet is connected with both of them in the two ways mentioned from the portion of Ḥesed and Gevurah which are in Tiferet, and from the portion of Tiferet which is in Ḥesed and Gevurah.

16. [The beginner] must also know that though we have previously stated that there is no Judgment in the three upper [sefirot], and that even Binah is removed from Judgment, as we have explained, nonetheless the Judgment of Gevurah is suspended in Binah. If Binah adds to it and influences Judgment, it is able to function, for the branch goes after the source. [However,] if Binah does not influence the Judgment in Gevurah, it has no power to execute. Now that which the rabbis have explained is clear, that in the innermost houses [of the divine] there is a grief which is related to the heart, and in the rest of the organs which are the outer houses there is not.[10]

17. [The beginner] must also know that the three first [sefirot] are thought of as one. That is, the [first three] qualities have three aspects in their unity. Firstly there is the matter of the [divine] Unity which is transmitted to each believer so that he should not divide [the Godhead] and think in terms of multiplicity in God, God forbid. Rather [the believer must assume that] the entire emanation

10. Cf. Ḥagigah 5b.

constitutes a complete unity. That which was said concerning its separation and demarcation is from our perspective and not [that of the sefirot], God forbid. Indeed, from our perspective this demarcation, consisting of the order of emanation, is one of two types.

[In the first,] the emanation is emanated generally, and most of the blessing does not depart for the world from the first three [sefirot]. Rather these three [sefirot] are considered as one, and their emanation does not depart for the world. This [situation] is called "friendship." Rather it is the union [of the sefirot] which causes emanation to come through the male-female principle, which is found between Ḥokhmah and Binah, which are the upper Father and Mother, or between Tiferet and Malkhut, the lower Father and Mother. This is the mystery of their union, imagined as the union of male and female, [but which actually signifies] something the human mind cannot comprehend.

This is a great matter which contains within itself [the secret] of a wondrous emanation in the existents and the souls. With respect to ourselves, [38a] this [union] may be interrupted also among the three first [sefirot] because of [our] sin. It is our responsibility to repair [the interruptions] and to continue [the emanation] and to unite [the sefirot] properly. With that this chapter is concluded.

3

18. [The beginner] must also know that it is not proper for a student [of Kabbalah] to inquire as to the essence of the three first [sefirot], which constitute intellect, wisdom, and understanding.[1] It is furthermore improper to investigate the hidden force which created all that exists.[2] Since He, His will and wisdom and understanding are one, and they are true qualities of His essence, it is not proper to inquire [into it]. However, from Ḥesed and Gevurah and below, there is no sin in investigating them, for they are qualities which have been emanated in order to direct the lower beings. One who increases his investigation into them is called industrious and will be rewarded. Similar to this [case] is that which is written, *You shall surely send forth the mother*—which is Binah[3]—*and the sons*[4] *you will take for yourself* (Deut. 22:7), to inquire and investigate. Thus also, *inquire now as to the first days* (Deut. 4:32).

19. [The beginner] must also know that the activities of Ḥesed are manifold. Nonetheless, we will mention some which will presently be made [understandable] to the reader. (1) Ḥesed ("Mercy") is, as its name implies, to help and succor man. It also [serves] to nullify the power of the Outside Ones[5] who accuse and vex man. Among the activities of this quality are also all the matters having to do with whiteness, like the stones whose color is white and whose virtues [derive from] Ḥesed. Among its actions is love.

1. In this enumeration, Keter is referred to as *sekhel*, i.e., "intellect."
2. This is a reference to Keter and Eyn Sof.
3. Binah, linked with Ḥokhmah, is the "mother" of all the lower sefirot.
4. The seven lower sefirot.
5. The forces of the *kelipah*.

Despite the fact that the arousal of love is from the Left side,[6] its major thrust and goal are contained in the Right side,[7] as is written, *I have loved you with an eternal love, therefore I have drawn you with mercy* (*ḥesed*) (Jer. 31:3). Among its actions, it draws a man to wisdom through the power of Ḥokhmah, which is above it on the right side. Among its actions it can include Gevurah within itself to execute Judgment, in which there is a small [admixture of] Mercy, as [in the case of] the drowning of the Egyptians in the Sea. This quality [of Ḥesed] possesses seventy-two bridges. This is hinted at in the seventy-two names contained in the verses *he journeyed . . . he came . . . he pitched . . .* (Exod. 19:2).[8]

20. [The beginner] must also know that among the actions of Gevurah are stern Judgment, exactly as its name [implies]. It is a lash to punish men. From it stem all the Outside forces which denounce and oppose [man]. Among its actions are all the matters which partake of the mystery of redness, the heat of fire, and the power of the stones that have a red color. Their virtue is to impose fear on the creatures. Also from this quality love is aroused, as we have explained. Wealth also derives from this quality with the aid of Binah, which is above it. Sustenance is also derived from this quality, and the witness [to this] is the table in the north.[9] Also, all hearing of prayer and cries is [effected] through this quality, though admittedly this occurs with the help of Binah.

21. [The beginner] must also know that among the actions of Tiferet are glory and majesty, as its name testifies. The reason is that majesty and beauty are a combination of white and red, as [the verse] states, *My beloved is white and red* (Song of Songs 5:10).

6. I.e., that of Gevurah.

7. I.e., that of Gedulah or Ḥesed.

8. Ḥesed equals 72 in gematria.

9. Cf. Mishnah, Zevaḥim 5:1, in which the most holy things were slaughtered on the north side of the altar.

Thus all the matters which are composed of red and white, fire and water, dryness and wetness, Judgment and Mercy, [combine] in the mystery of this quality. Thus the greenish color of an egg yolk [exists] among the precious stones. All of these are influenced by [Tiferet], and their virtue is in its power. Also dependent upon it are the Torah and its study. Also the [begetting of] sons depends upon the supernal qualities [sefirot], and its true locus is in this quality. Also the manna used to descend to Israel from the midst of this quality. Upon [Tiferet] also depends the matter of the begetting of souls, which is the recondite meaning of the union of this quality with that of Malkhut. This [union] is something which is to be found in these [two] qualities and in Ḥokhmah and Binah, [but] which is not to be found in all the other qualities.

22. In the matter of the aforementioned union, the reader must know that, aside from Ḥokhmah and Binah, which are called "Husband" and "Wife," "Father" and "Mother," and [whose union] is similar to physical union and mating, there is not to be found [union] between male and female except through the intermediation of the covenant of pudenda.[10] Thus on high these two qualities [Ḥokhmah and Binah] unite in the mystery of the primordial Da'at,[11] which is in the middle between "Father" and "Mother." Its existence is in *the path which the bird of prey does not know* (Job 28:7). The result of [39a] this union is the existence and renewal of the sefirot, which are continually renewed through their root, which is sunk in the depths of Binah and Ḥokhmah and also continues in the mystery of the soul, which is from Binah. This will be explained in the *Tikkunim*, with God's help.[12] Likewise the

10. The generative power of human beings is thought of as an earthly counterpart to the acts of sefirotic generation described.

11. Thus Da'at is an intermediary factor between Ḥokhmah and Binah.

12. I have been unable to identify the source in *Tikkunei Zohar*.

crown with which the Mother crowned the children on the day of their wedding comes [from this], as it is written, *Go out and see, O daughters of Zion* (Song of Songs 3:11). However, all union requires an arousal from below, and the arousal of Binah [stems] from Malkhut, as Rabbi Simeon bar Yoḥai, peace upon him, explained.

23. The manner of this union may be found in [the relationship of] Tiferet and Malkhut, which are male and female, bridegroom and bride, lower father and mother, son and daughter to the Upper [sefirot], king and queen, king and matrona, Holy One, blessed be He, and His Shekhinah, king in his palace. All this metaphorizes the aforementioned matter. Nonetheless, their union requires an arousal from the souls of the righteous in the lower world.

Now a prior aspect of this union includes the aspect of embrace which occurs at the hand of Ḥesed and Gevurah. This mystery is hinted at in the verse, *his left hand is under my head* (Song of Songs 2:6, 8:3)—this indicates that the emanation of Ḥesed is influenced by Tiferet and unites with it. Afterwards Tiferet continues [the emanation] to Gevurah and unites with it. Thus the Bridegroom is united on his two arms. After that he receives the Bride with his left hand, and Gevurah extends into Malkhut and influences it. After that, the emanation of Ḥesed, the right arm, continues to her, and thus the left hand is below and the right hand embraces above. This is the mystery of *his left hand.*

Also accompanying this [union] is the aspect of the kiss. There is no doubt that the kiss is the clinging of spirit to spirit. It is the mystery of the union of the inner essence of the [sefirotic] qualities illuminating one another. This is the mystery of the mouth. It is the essence of Malkhut in Tiferet and similarly [Tiferet] in Malkhut. This matter is lengthy and it is explained in the 'Idra.[13]

13. Zohar III, 127b-145a. Cf. especially 140b, where there is a discussion of the mouth.

The subject of the benefits deriving from this union are very great. From it derive male souls from the Male side and female souls from the Female side. Moreover, accompanying this union are [the sefirot] Neẓaḥ and Hod, these [39b] two testicles of the male [appearing] together with Yesod, which is the mystery of the covenant and union.

24. Behold, I have explained two unions of these four qualities. Now these unions may be explained by two [divine] Names twice. Thus Father = YHWH, Mother = Ehyeh. Their union together will result in this [divine] Name: YAHHVIHH. This is the mystery of the union of Ḥokhmah and Binah, He to the right and She to the left. They possess three places for the union in the mystery of their light, which spreads through the sefirot from top to bottom. They are in Keter together with the mystery of Da'at, and also below in Tiferet and farther below in Yesod.

In this manner [also is affected the union of Tiferet and] Malkhut. They are Son = YHWH and Daughter = Adonai. Their union together results in this [divine] Name: YAHDVNHI. They possess three places for [their] union in the mystery of their light, which spreads through the sefirot from below to above. These are in Yesod, in Tiferet, and in Da'at. In Malkhut these four names are united like this: YAY, AHHHH, HDVYNH, HHY. This indicates the union of three lights: right, left, and center whether ascending or descending.

25. The actions of Neẓaḥ, Hod, and Yesod are close to the actions of Tiferet, Gedulah, and Gevurah, since they derive sustenance from them: Neẓaḥ from Ḥesed, Yesod from Tiferet, and Hod from Gevurah. However, together with their deriving sustenance they also receive emanation from Tiferet to both of them as well as the emanation of Ḥesed and Gevurah with Yesod. Because of this it is sometimes considered "right" and sometimes "left."

Also, these three participate in the aforementioned union, so much so that they are called the two male testicles and the mother. Thus their actions are [concerted] together to ripen the seed of the male and the female. They are called heavens (*shekhakim*), for they grind [*shekhakin*] manna for the Righteous and for Righteousness.[14] They possess one [divine] name which is indivisible. It is the name *Ẓeva'ot.*

26. All the sefirot may be distinguished in two ways. Firstly they can be divided into triads. First of all, Keter, Ḥokhmah, and Binah. Secondly, Ḥesed, Gevurah, and Tiferet. Thirdly, Neẓaḥ, Hod, and Yesod, with Malkhut the sum of all. The second manner of distinguishing [the sefirot involves] the three [sefirot] of the right side, [40a] which are Ḥokhmah, Ḥesed, and Neẓaḥ. The three [sefirot] of the left side are Binah, Gevurah, and Hod. The three central [sefirot] are Keter, Tiferet, and Yesod. Malkhut is the sum of all. It is also well to say that Keter above is like Malkhut [below], and Da'at [thus would hold a] central [position] in place of Keter. This will be explained in the Book *Pardes [Rimmonim].*

14. Cf. Ḥagigah 12b.

4

[Sec. 9] 27. [The beginner] must also know that there is a balancing force between the two extremes, that is, between Love and Judgment. The balancing force is Mercy.[1] Now there are extremes in three places, each of which has a balancing force. The first [pair of] opposites is between Neẓaḥ and Hod, and the balancing force is Yesod. The second opposition is between Ḥesed and Gevurah, and the balancing force is Tiferet. The third opposition is between Ḥokhmah and Binah, and the balancing force is Tiferet in the mystery of Da'at.[2] This does not mean that Ḥokhmah and Binah actually constitute [the qualities of] Love and Judgment. However, [the matter] partakes of the mystery of the Judgments which awaken from Binah.[3] Therefore Da'at, which stems from Keter, is the balancing force. The matter of this balance involves being midway between the two extremes and being an intermediary of peace between them.

[Sec. 10] 28. [The beginner] must also know that colors are ascribed to the [sefirotic] qualities according to their actions. Thus whiteness is ascribed to Mercy, and redness to Judgment, and the like, as is well known. Regarding Keter there are those who say that it has no color at all, while others say that whiteness in the extreme would be appropriate for it. Still others attribute the color black to it. These three colors symbolize its three characteristics.

1. Mercy represents love which is balanced by judgment.
2. Da'at often forms a triad with Ḥokhmah and Binah.
3. Of the uppermost sefirot, Binah is the origin of judgment.

First there is the characteristic of Emanator, in which He is black. Secondly, in terms of Himself, since He is not revealed to the emanated, no color could define Him. Thirdly, in terms of His influence of Mercy on the rest of the sefirot, He [partakes of] the mystery of whiteness.

Moreover, there are three shades of the color of darkness. The first is absolute darkness with no [admixture of] light. This is found many times [40b] in the Zohar. Secondly, [darkness] comes to indicate the removal of light and is not to be perceived like the [former] darkness, as [Scripture] states: *He made darkness His hiding place* (Ps. 18:12). Thus they have [merely] not yet seen the clear light of the heavens. Thirdly, [it] teaches concerning the aspect of the Female which is black, [and] pale. These three aspects exist in Keter. The first is the disappearance of its light. The second is the absence of its light in relation to its Emanator. The third contains an aspect of femininity, as will be explained.

29. [The beginner] must also know that the color of Ḥokhmah is the chief of all the colors, just as [Ḥokhmah] is the beginning of all action. The development of the colors [commences] from Ḥokhmah, and thus its color is blue, which is the beginning of the development of color from blackness. Black develops into dark blue. Some have interpreted that its color is that of the sapphire, which is the beginning of all colors and is near to the color blue. The color of Binah is green like the grass. The reason [for this] is that this color contains the colors of red and white, which are perceived together, that is, Gedulah, Gevurah, and Tiferet. It also contains the color blue, which is from Ḥokhmah. Thus we have a coming together of all these qualities in Binah.

30. The color of Ḥesed is white. Not the whitest white like Keter, but rather a white which is nearly blue. It is the color of silver. Gevurah possesses three colors. The first color is black,

which derives from its aspect of Gehinnom,[4] which blackens the faces of the creatures. Second is the color red, which [signifies] good Judgment which pleases God and man in order to arouse the [sefirotic] union. Third is the color blue, which is related to the Judgment which proceeds by way of holiness to Malkhut. There is yet a fourth color, the color of gold, which is common to Binah and Gevurah in the mystery of the joysome wine which proceeds to Gevurah from Binah.

The color of Tiferet [was described] above. They ascribed to it [the color] sapphire in the extension of Da'at. In its revealed aspect of determination, it includes white and red—that is, the green of an egg yolk, in truth. Now Tiferet [41a] includes the color[s] of Ḥesed and Gevurah in one of two [manners]. It is either above them in the mystery of Da'at, which includes them in their roots or in its lower aspect, that is, the mixture of red and white. It also possesses the color purple, which includes five colors. They are the mystery [of the angels] Uriel, Refael, Gavriel, Mikhael, and Nuriel.[5]

31. Neẓaḥ [possesses the color] red shading to white, for it is mostly mercy because of its orientation to the side of Ḥesed. Hod is white shading to red because it is mostly Judgment due to its orientation to the side of Gevurah. Yesod has as its color a mixture of white shading to red and red shading to white. There are those who interpreted that its color was sapphire-like, since it receives all the colors of the sefirot. For this reason, there are those who interpreted that [its] color contained all the colors.

Malkhut contains all the colors. Sometimes it possesses the color black, sometimes the color blue. Black [stems] from the side of the "outside" ones. Blue [serves Malkhut] to protect her from

4. I.e., hell.

5. The Hebrew word for "purple," *argaman*, refers in an acrostic to the five angels mentioned (note that Uriel begins with an *alef*).

them. Its color, as well, is that of *fine linen and purple* (Prv. 31:22). These are the colors of its aspects. However, its essential color [stems from] the light of Tiferet. It possesses the color of white light, like that of the moon, which reflects the sun's [light]. It also possesses the color green, which is an aspect between white from the side of Tiferet and blue from the side of Gevurah. This refers to the rising of the dawn, [when] she is situated between Gevurah and Tiferet.

32. [The beginner] must also know that the essence of these colors is [related] to the [sefirotic] qualities in Malkhut, just as the essence of their actions is in her. Thus the name YHWH has no color at all, and the essence of the colors is in the name Adonai. Indeed, the light from above, which exhibits an obscure color which is Malkhut below, is the mystery of the light of YHWH and the obscurity in which the colors—Adonai—are contained.

[Sec. 11] 33. [The beginner] must also know that above, in Keter, may be found the existence of all the sefirot. These [existences] are called by Kabbalists the ten brightnesses. They are included in three, just as the sefirot are encompassed in Ḥesed, Judgment, and Mercy. They hide their branches [41b] in their roots, which are Neẓaḥ in Ḥesed and Ḥesed in Ḥokhmah. Thus [too], Hod [disappears] in Gevurah, and Gevurah in Binah. Thus [too], Malkhut and Yesod [merge] with Tiferet, and all of them [merge] into Keter. They constitute the mystery of Keter, Ḥokhmah, Binah in Keter. They are designated primordial light, the burnished light, the clear light. On the order of the recurrent light, [they are] Knowledge, Understanding, and Intelligence. Those who mention them, primordial [light], clear [light], or burnished [light], refer to Keter, Ḥokhmah, and Binah. The comprehension of these sefirot with these brightnesses is very difficult and sublime. These [sefirot] constitute the root of the roots of the sefirot which are Keter,

Ḥokhmah, and Binah. These three [sefirot] are also to be found in Malkhut, since she is the pattern of the higher [sefirot].

[Sec. 12] 34. Ḥokhmah also possesses aspects [of itself] which are called "pathways." There are thirty-two of them.[6] Their existence consists of the ten sefirot together and the twelve borders of diagonals and the seven qualities for special providence which they possess and the three first [sefirot], which are higher for a greater [form of] providence than the previous one. These "pathways" have names given [them] which are known and explained. They correspond to the thirty-two [mentions of the name] Elohim in the section Bereshit. The seal of Genesis is at their hand.

[Sec. 13] 35. Binah also possesses aspects which are called "gates."[7] There are fifty of them, corresponding to the fifty times that the exodus from Egypt is mentioned in the Torah. Their [number is explained by] the seven sefirot multiplied seven times, equaling forty-nine, while Binah herself completes the total of fifty. Thus [also] five sefirot which include the ten equal fifty. This matter is expanded upon in the book *Pardes [Rimmonim]*. Since Binah is the root of the [sefirotic] qualities, the seven qualities in their generality were sought in her.

[Sec. 14] 36. [The beginner] must also know that the actions of [the sefirotic world] of holiness and spirituality are not like the deeds of lowly and inadequate human beings. For when a human being acts and performs any action, then the thing which is acted upon acquires the form required, and necessarily loses its former form and nature, and transforms from one existence to another, [42a] while the former existence of that thing will no longer be remembered.

6. Cf. *Sefer Yeẓirah* 1:1.
7. Cf. Rosh ha-Shanah 21b.

This is not the case with the sefirot. [Despite] all the things which develop out of them, their previous existence will not cease. Rather they will develop from one existence to another. For example, when the sefirot were submerged within Keter, all of them were present there. Even after their emanation, their existence remains there, for [Keter] does not cease to exist and will not change. This is also [the rule] concerning their emanation from Ḥokhmah and for all their subjects. Thus the [sefirotic] qualities themselves also have their existence in this manner. They exchange and multiply infinitely. The reader may find this difficult. We have expanded its explanation in the book *Pardes [Rimmonim]*.

Similarly the Qualities possess existence [in terms of] ten and seven and five and six and four and three. All [this] is a mystery of the changing light according to its meaning, [such] that their existence is not changed whether they constitute six together or five or whatever. Nonetheless, each [sefirotic] quality [possesses] an aspect in which it is inclusive of six [sefirot], which is not exactly the aspect of its being inclusive of seven or of ten. For each constitutes a different existence. Thus one existence may come to it from the side of Ḥokhmah, and a second existence may come to her from the side of Binah. With this the chapter is completed.

5

[Sec. 15] 37. Just as the light of the sefirot spreads out and emanates directly from above to below like [natural] light, [from] Keter [to] Ḥokhmah, Binah, Gedulah, Gevurah, Tiferet, Neẓaḥ, Hod, Yesod, [and] Malkhut, so the light, after it descends to its [proper] place, returns and spreads from below to above: Keter in Malkhut, and Ḥokhmah in Yesod, and Binah in Hod, and Ḥesed in Neẓaḥ, and Gevurah in Tiferet, and Tiferet in Gevurah, and Neẓaḥ in Ḥesed, and Hod in Binah, and Yesod in Ḥokhmah, and Malkhut in Keter. This is the mystery of the light which returns from below to above. It is the secret of the reversed light which strikes the mirror and returns to its source. This matter may also be seen with [the sefirot between] Ḥokhmah and Malkhut in the mystery of the special providence [exercised] over [these] nine [sefirotic] qualities in the elevation of Keter. [It also may be seen in the sefirot] from Ḥesed to Yesod [42b] in the conduct of the six "directions"[1] by themselves and mixed together. Between each [sefirotic] quality there is a connection which goes [both] up and down. Within the quality itself there is a part [going] from bottom to top, and [another] part [going] from top to bottom.

[Sec. 16] 38. [The beginner] must also know that [all] existents which stem from Him until the lowest point are divided into four divisions.[2]

1. The six "directions" (North, South, East, West, Up, and Down) refer to the six sefirot between Gedulah and Yesod. Cf. *Sefer Yeẓirah* 1:5.

2. For a convenient schematization of these four divisions, see Aryeh Kaplan, *Sefer Yezirah: The Book of Creation* (York Beach, Maine: Samuel Weiser, 1990), p. 42, table 7.

The first division is that of "Emanation." It consists of the ten emanated sefirot among which the light of Eyn Sof spreads. The second division is the realm of the Throne of Glory, which is called "Creation." The light of the sefirot [of Emanation] spreads in it. The [sefirot of this division] are called the sefirot of Creation, not [those of] the "throne." However, the light is that of the ten sefirot, while the light of Eyn Sof is garbed in them through the emanated light. The third division is the realm of the ten classes of angels who constitute the "Palaces."[3] The light of the ten sefirot spreads also among them through the light of the ten sefirot of Creation. This [division] is called "Formation," and the sefirot which spread among them are called the ten sefirot of Formation. The light of Eyn Sof is garbed [within them] in the emanated [sefirotic] light. The fourth division is the realm of the firmaments and all the lowly material world. [This division] is called "Making." It consists of ten firmaments. The light of the sefirot spreads among them, and they are called the ten sefirot of Making, which consists of the spreading of holiness in the midst of the material matter in which the "outside" ones rule.

[Thus] these [four divisions] are called Emanation, Creation, Formation, and Making. Their acronym is ABYA. Thus Emanation is above Creation, and Creation is above Formation, and Formation is above Making. These four divisions may be found in Emanation, and in Creation, and in Formation, and in Making, since the degrees descend from cause to caused.

[Sec. 17] 39. [The beginner] must also know that the [sefirah] Neẓaḥ, during the six days of creation, derived sustenance from

3. The reference is to the "Palaces" (*Heikhalot*) of the angelic realm. On the early Jewish "Palace" literature, see Gershom Scholem, *Jewish Gnosticism, Merkabah Mysticism and the Talmudic Tradition* (New York: Jewish Theological Seminary, 1965).

the side of Gevurah,[4] and Hod from [the side of] Ḥesed, in the mystery of the mingling of the Qualities. Since because of [Adam's] sin the [sefirotic] connections have been confused,[5] none of the men of valor were able to repair this defect until the righteous one, Jacob [43a] our father, [took] Judgment upon himself, saying, *If Esau comes* below and his [angelic] "minister" above[6] to arouse Judgment *on the one camp* (Gen. 32:9), [namely,] the female Hod. ([She is called] the captain of the hosts, [since] camp and hosts are the same. Thus the fact that Hod's strength was weak like a woman['s] is not difficult [to comprehend].) Now [we understand] *and strikes it* [in the sense that "Esau"] weakened the strength of the [sefirotic] stature in general. This is hinted at by [the additional letter] *vav* in the name [of Jacob in the verse] *truth unto Jacob* (Mic. 7:20). Thus he destroyed his mercy. *And the remaining camp*, which is Neẓaḥ, strengthens itself as a remnant to grasp on to the quality of Ḥesed. Thus it was that the minister of Esau touched the thigh of Jacob and immediately the order of nourishment was changed and Hod returned, influenced from the side of Gevurah[7] in the mystery of *My comeliness was turned in me into corruption* (Dan. 10:8). Neẓaḥ was [thus] weakened until King David, peace upon him, came and repaired it with his melodies[8] so that it might derive nourishment from the side of Ḥesed. This is the mystery of [the verse] *in Your right hand is bliss forevermore* (*neẓaḥ*) (Ps. 16:11).

4. In the "normative" sefirotic order, Neẓaḥ is found on the "side" of Gedulah (Ḥesed), while Hod is on the side of Gevurah.

5. This is an expression of the idea that sin on the earthly plane causes "disruption" in the order of the sefirot on high.

6. Cf. Rashi on Gen. 32:25.

7. The "touching" apparently restored the sefirotic state of "confusion." Cf. n. 4 above.

8. The psalms.

After this introduction, how much sweeter than honey is [the passage] found in some midrashim that Michael, the angel of Mercy, was the one to touch the thigh of Jacob,[9] for [both] this and that come after Ḥesed agreed to push away the quality of Hod from beside it so that its [characteristic of] Judgment would not commingle. Then, when Ḥesed was grasped very well and it was tied up on the right [side],[10] Hod also was tied to the left [side] in order to reprove with equity the kings of Judah and all the people of the land so as to put an end to sin and to stop transgression. At that time, which was one of [divine] will, King David, peace upon him, merited that His will be done to arrange the [sefirotic] qualities as in olden days in the mystery of *Your priests will garb themselves with righteousness, and Your pious ones will rejoice* (Ps. 132:9), which is explained in the Zohar.[11] Thus it is destined to renew itself permanently in the days of the Messiah.

[Sec. 18] 40. [The beginner] must also know that the emanation of Malkhut and Tiferet in union stems from the height of the degrees beginning from Ḥokhmah. This is the mystery of the dual face[12] in which they were created. However, within Ḥokhmah they constitute the *vav* prior to the *daled* in the order of the completion of the [spelling of] *yod* in the [divine] Name.[13] They emanate and come in to Binah as *daled* before *vav*. In Binah, through Ḥesed, Malkhut is separated from Tiferet and Malkhut remains in Ḥokhmah-within-Binah. Tiferet emanates, and afterwards [43b] *And the Lord built* (*banah*), Binah, *the rib*, Malkhut, *which he took from the man*, Ḥokhmah, *and brought it to the man*, Tiferet (Gen. 2:22). *And there*

9. Cf. Bereshit Rabbah 78:1. In the Zohar, Michael symbolizes the sefirah Gedulah/Ḥesed (I, 98b-99a).

10. I.e., its "proper" side.

11. Zohar I, 148a.

12. I.e. a hermaphrodite. Cf. Eruvin 18a, Bereshit Rabbah 8:1.

13. The word *yod* is spelled out with three letters: *yod*, *vav*, and *daled*.

was still not [a help meet for him] (Gen. 2:20)—this is the mystery of diminution.[14] However, Malkhut was below Tiferet, with both of them deriving sustenance from [the side of] Judgment from Gevurah and Binah. Similarly, Ḥesed [derived its sustenance] from Gedulah and Binah. Tiferet forced Malkhut to the side of Mercy, for he is "below" relative to Mercy. Then [Malkhut] criticized and said, "It is impossible," since her intention was that Malkhut should work [in the sphere of] Judgment and Tiferet in Mercy, and that Tiferet would not force Malkhut to the side of Mercy. Then we say to her, "Go and diminish yourself." Thus they subtracted from its light, and whereas previously she had been at the seventh rung, she descended to the tenth [rung] because of the diminution of her merit.

[Sec. 19] 41. [The beginner] must also know that while the [divine] names which may not be erased[15] are numerous, and while there are ten names [corresponding to] the ten sefirot, there exists one general name for all the sefirot. It is the four-letter name YDVD. The meaning is that Y = Ḥokhmah, H = Binah, V includes six sefirot,[16] and the final H = Malkhut. Eyn Sof disappears into Keter, and its light spreads in these four letters from *yod* to *heh*, and from *heh* to *vav*, and from *vav* to the final *heh*. However, this name will become full with ten letters to hint at this. These [letters are] *yod, heh, vav, heh*.[17] The punctuation of the Name also indicates the ten sefirot in this manner: YODEVADE. The *ḥolem*[18]

14. The reference is to the diminution of the moon. Cf. Bereshit Rabbah 6:3. The moon is a symbol of the sefirah Malkhut.

15. Cf. Sifrei on Deuteronomy, piska 61, on Deut. 12:4. Cf. also Shevuot 35a.

16. The numerical value of *vav* is six. The six sefirot are those from Gedulah to Hod.

17. The letters are spelled out in full, thus equaling ten. Cf. n. 13 above.

18. Hebrew vowel with the *o* sound.

[indicates] Keter, the *kamaẓ*[19] [indicates] Tiferet, the first [*segol*][20] [indicates] Ḥokhmah, Binah, Ḥesed, and the last [*segol*] indicates Neẓaḥ, Hod, Yesod. The dot in the *kamaẓ* [hints] at Gevurah, and the letters themselves are Malkhut. [Thus the Name is] expanded to hint at the mystery of Ten. [This is] also [true concerning] the *yods* in this manner: YOD HY VYV HY. This name is [contained] in Ḥokhmah-within-Keter. The expanded name with *'alefs* is within the actual Ḥokhmah. However, since each of the sefirot contains the ten [sefirot], the four[-lettered] Name is found in each of them. Thus YAHAVAHA, [voweled] entirely with *kamaẓ* is in Keter, [44a] YADAVADA, [voweled] entirely with *pataḥ*,[21] is in Ḥokhmah, YEDEVEDE, [voweled] entirely with *ẓere*,[22] is in Binah, YEDEVEDE, [voweled] entirely with *segol*, is in Ḥesed. YIDIVIDI, [voweled] entirely with *shva*,[23] is in Gevurah, YODOVODO, [voweled] entirely with *ḥolem*,[24] is in Tiferet YIDIVIDI, [voweled] entirely with *ḥirik*,[25] is in Neẓaḥ, YUDUVUDU, [voweled] entirely with *shuruk*,[26] is in Hod, YUDUD, [voweled] entirely in *shuruk*, is in Yesod. Malkhut [goes] with the Name of the plain [unvoweled] letters since she is made up of all of the [sefirot] and acts according to the influence of each and every sefirah upon it. Therefore she is voweled according to her [source of] sustenance.

[Sec. 20] 42. There exist "palaces" and "garments" for these Names. They are the ten [divine] Names which are not to be

19. Hebrew vowel with the *a* sound.
20. Hebrew vowel with the *e* sound.
21. Hebrew vowel with the *a* sound.
22. Hebrew vowel with the *e* sound.
23. Hebrew vowel signifying either a short *e* or else no sound.
24. I.e., *o*.
25. Hebrew vowel with the *e* sound.
26. Hebrew vowel with the *u* sound.

erased. The Name for Keter is Ehyeh.[27] This [Name] indicates the sublimity of Keter, which is to be revealed in the future but which has not [yet] been revealed at all.[28] Therefore this Name is pronounced according to its letters, since its pronunciation teaches its sublimity. This Name appertains to Keter from the aspect of Binah [inherent] within it. From the aspect of Ḥokhmah [inherent] within it, its name is the four[-letter] Name. It itself has neither name nor vowel.

Ḥokhmah's [Name] is Yah. This Name indicates the cooperation of Ḥokhmah and Binah together. The name of Binah is YIHEVID, which indicates the influence of Judgment and Mercy from Binah and also indicates [the fact that] Tiferet, which is called YDVD, emanated from her. Malkhut is called Elokim. The Name for Ḥesed is El. This Name indicates the spreading of Ḥesed from Ḥokhmah and also indicates in the form of the *'alef* the completion of the three branches in Ḥesed, which are Ḥesed and Gevurah in the two *yods*, and Tiferet [in the] *vav*.[29] The measure of both of them is in the center. It also indicates that it encompasses the unity and causes it, for the *vav* [indicates] Tiferet and Malkhut and Yesod, [which] are included in the lower *yod*. The three first [sefirot] shine there in the upper *yod*. *Lamed* indicates Binah, which influences directly over all.

The [divine] Name for Gevurah is 'Elohim. This name indicates Binah, which is called "Who," [along] with the three Patriarchs,[30]

27. Cf. Exod. 3:14.

28. Cf. Zohar III, 152a, in which the righteous, in time to come, will be destined to look upon the "soul of the soul" of the Torah, which is identified with Keter.

29. *Alef* (א) is thus seen as a combination of two *yods* and a *vav*.

30. The three sefirot, Gedulah, Gevurah, and Tiferet, are identified with the three patriarchs, Abraham, Isaac, and Jacob. Cf. Isa. 40:26: "See *who* has created *these*." The implication is that Binah begot the three sefirotic "patriarchs."

who are called "Those" (*eleh*). This Name may be found in Gevurah and in Binah and in Malkhut. It is all a hint at "those" three, [which are] places of Judgment.

The [divine] Name of Tiferet is YIDAVD, which is indicated [by the verse] *Only the Lord had a delight (ḥashak) in your fathers* (Deut. 10:15). [44b] *Ḥashak* [is an acronym for the vowels] *ḥolem, shva, kamaẓ*. The four letters indicate the two crowns which succeed Father and Mother, i.e., *Yod* = Ḥokhmah, *heh* = Binah. Both of them are included in *vav*, which influences Malkhut.

The [divine] Name for Neẓaḥ and Hod is *Ẓeva'ot*, which teaches that they continue the strength of the Male through Yesod to the Female [Malkhut]. [The divine Name] for Yesod is Shaddai, which indicates its supplying of overflow to the Female. Also, the emanation continues up to Yesod. Here [God] said, "Enough [of emanation]!" to His world,[31] for Malkhut is above it, as we have explained. There are those who have ascribed to it the name "Living God." This is explained in the Book *Pardes [Rimmonim]*.

In Malkhut the [divine] Name Adonai indicates many matters which are explained [in *Pardes Rimmonim*]. These four letters are a "garment" for the four letters of the four-letter Name [which when combined looks] like this: YAHDVNHY. With this the chapter is completed.

31. Cf. the etymology of Shaddai in Ḥagigah 12a: "I [God] am the one who said to the world, 'Enough!'"

6

[Sec. 21] 43. [The beginner] must also know that there are holy Names inferior to these. They are similar to appellations for them. [Thus] they have ascribed to Keter the Name Araryta, and to Ḥokhmah the twenty-two [Hebrew] letters with [the suffix] *yah*, like this: *ayah*, *byah*, etc. This [Name] designates the three first [sefirot] together: Khuzu Behokhsaz Khuzu. To Ḥesed belongs the seventy-two letter Name which comes out of the verses *He traveled . . . he came . . . he pitched* (Exod. 19:2). It contains 216 letters like the numerical [equivalent] of *aryeh* in Ḥesed. Gevurah has the forty-two letter Name which comes out of [the verses] from *In the beginning* (Gen. 1:1) to the *bet* in *bohu* ("void"), [equaling] forty-two letters. They constitute seven Names corresponding to the seven sefirot.

Tiferet possesses the Name of twenty-two [letters] which comes out from *May the Lord bless you* (Num. 6:24). Neẓaḥ has another Name of twenty-two [letters]. Hod has a Name which stems from the verse *You will fear the Lord your God* (Deut. 6:13, 10:20). Yesod possesses twelve permutations of the four[-letter] Name. Malkhut has the Name Metatron.[1] I have explained the meaning of these Names at length in the book *Pardes [Rimmonim]*.

The sefirot also possess appellations which serve as a garment [concealing] the Names which are not to be erased. They are appellations of the actions of the sefirot and their relations. It is not, [45a] as many have thought, [that they are named] by agreement of the sages or by chance. [The Names] are, rather, ascribed

1. On the angel Metatron, see Scholem, *Kabbalah*, pp. 377-381.

to the sefirot according to their characteristics. Many appellations have been attached to one quality for the reason that sometimes it derives its sustenance from above from the side of Judgment, at which time one Name [is appropriate], and at other times it will derive sustenance from [the side of] Mercy and has another name. An example of this is that Ḥokhmah has one Name in its own right and a second Name due to its influence over Ḥesed and a third Name due to its receiving [emanation] from Keter. The Names differ according to its receipt from the aspect of Keter and differ further according to its influence over Ḥesed. Thus in this way [its Name changes] with the change of aspects.

[Sec. 22] 44. [The beginner] must also know that the righteous have the power to constitute a chariot for the Qualities in the mystery of the continuity of their souls and actions in this world and their orientation to one of the [divine] aspects and one of the qualities. Thus Abraham [was termed] a man of Ḥesed, Isaac a man of Gevurah, and Jacob the master of Tiferet; Moses was the master of Neẓaḥ, and Aaron the master of Hod. [There are] more [correspondences] in a different manner: Aaron [could be considered] a man of Ḥesed; Moses the man of Da'at, which is subumed within Tiferet[2]; Joseph [was] master of Yesod, and thus [also] Palti ben Laish and Boaz and Solomon. Solomon relates to the mystery of Da'at in its general existence in Yesod. There are many similar [correspondences] in which David is the master of Malkhut and thus most of the righteous kings. We have dealt with this matter at length in the book *Pardes [Rimmonim]*, with God's help.

However, these special men who are called by name, who are the foundations of every generation in the generality of the stature of emanation, are: Adam, Noah, Shem, Ḥokhmah, Binah, Da'at;

2. On the position of Da'at within the sefirotic system, see Scholem, *Kabbalah*, pp. 107 ff.

Abraham, Isaac, Jacob, Ḥesed, Paḥad,[3] Tiferet; Moses, Aaron, Pinḥas, and David, Neẓaḥ, Hod, Yesod, Malkhut. All of them [partake] of the roots of the souls which pertain to the complete Adam in the wings of the Shekhinah, *mother of all living* [cf. Gen. 3:20]. From this [source stem] kings, righteous men, seers, prophets, men of truth, heroes, pious men, understanding men, wise men, the heads of the thousands of Israel.

45. [The beginner] must also know that [45b] in Tiferet there are twelve diagonal borders. These are the upper southern border, the lower southern border, the southeastern border, the southwestern border, totaling four. Also the upper northern border, the lower northern border, the northwestern border, the northeastern border, totaling four. Also the upper eastern border, the lower eastern border, the upper western border, and the lower western border, totaling four. They constitute twelve, corresponding to the twelve upper lights. They possess twelve existences. To them the twelve tribes of Israel constitute a chariot. The explanation of this at length [may be found] in the book *Pardes [Rimmonim]*, with God's help.

3. Cf. Gen. 31:42.

Part VII

A Brief Explanation of Some [Divine] Appellations

These are [Names] that *a wise man will hear and increase knowledge* (Prov. 1:5). Brevity in this [subject] will not satisfy the yearning soul. [It constitutes] but a modest beginning to teach the ways of our sanctified language, which in its entirety hints at upper [forces].[1] We have expatiated [on this] in the book *Pardes [Rimmonim]*.[2]

Letter *Alef*

Av ("Father") relates to Keter and also to Ḥokhmah.

Av ha-Emunah ("Father of Faith") relates to Keter and Ḥokhmah from the side of Malkhut and Binah.

Av ha-Raḥaman ("Father of Mercy") [relates to] Tiferet from the side of Keter.

Abir ("Mighty One"). Tiferet in a filial [relationship] with Malkhut. It has many aspects.

Avanim Mefulamot ("Viscous Stones"). In Ḥesed and sometimes in the corresponding *kelipah*.

Avne Tohu ("Stones of the Void"). In Ḥesed on the aforementioned [*kelipah*] side.

Avus ("Crib"). The place for deriving life from Malkhut.

Avak ("Dust"). Appellation of the *kelipah*.

Avak Rokhel ("Powder of the Merchant"). In Binah and in Yesod.

Ever ("Member, Male Organ"). Yesod.

1. Cf. Naḥmanides, who stated, in the introduction to his commentary on the Torah, that the Torah in its entirety is a divine Name.

2. *Pardes Rimmonim*, sec. 23.

Abraham. Ḥesed. [46a]

Agudah ("Bunch"). All the emanation by implication.

Egoz ("Nut"). Malkhut with the *kelipot* and Yesod.

Agan ("Basin"). Malkhut when she is full.

Ed ("Vapor"). Malkhut

Adon ("Master"). Malkhut and Yesod.

Adir. ("Majestic"). Binah and Gevurah.

Aderet ("Mantle"). Malkhut from the side of Gevurah.

Adam ("Man"). Ḥokhmah and Tiferet and all the emanation.

Adamah ("Earth"). Malkhut from the side of Judgment.

Admoni ("Ruddy"). Hod.

Adonai ("Lord"). Malkhut.

Adrikhal ("Architect"). Malkhut.

Ahavah ("Love"). It begins from Gevurah and ends in Ḥesed. It is Malkhut.

Ahah ("Alas"). The *alef* [is] Keter and the two *heh*s [are] Binah and Malkhut.

Ohel Moed ("Tent of Meeting"). Malkhut as dwelling place of Tiferet.

Oy ("Woe"). Tiferet retreats to Keter for ill.

Avir ("Air"). Tiferet and Keter; the union of Ḥokhmah and Binah.

Okhel ("Food"). The Righteous [Yesod].

Omen ("Tutor"). Yesod.

Aven ("Evil"). The *kelipah*. Thus with any form of iniquity or deceit.

Ofan ("Wheel"). Gedulah. The wheels of the chariot: Neẓaḥ, Hod, Yesod, and Malkhut.

Or ("Light"). In Tiferet, Ḥesed, and Binah.

Oraḥ ("Path"). From Keter to Tiferet. If it is crooked, [it refers to] the "outside" ones.

Ot ("Sign"). Yesod and sometimes in Malkhut.

Az ("Then"). The union of Ḥokhmah and Binah and also the union of Tiferet in Malkhut.

Ezov ("Hyssop"). The Righteous One influences Malkhut.

A" ("Brother"). Tiferet in relation to Malkhut from the side of Ḥesed, which includes [all the sefirot] until Yesod, which are nine.

Eḥad ("One" [masc.]). Tiferet inclusive of the nine [sefirot]; with Malkhut four.

Aḥor ("Behind"). Malkhut.

Aḥar ha-Devarim ("After the Things"). The *kelipah* and the accusers.

Aḥarit ("End"). Binah.

Aḥarit ha-Yamim ("End of Days"). Malkhut.

Aḥat ("One" [fem.]). Binah, Ḥokhmah, and Keter.

Atad ("Thorn Bush"). From the side of Rigorous Judgment and Gevurah. [46b]

Ei ("Where"). Ḥokhmah and Binah.

Ayin ("Nothing"). Keter inclusive of Ḥokhmah and Binah.

Ayelet ha-Shaḥar and *Ayelet Ahavim* ("Morning Star" and "Lovely Woman"). Malkhut.

Eyn Sof ("Without End"). Cause of all Causes.

Eyk (short for *Eyn Ketz*, "Without Finish"). Keter, Ḥokhmah, Binah or Keter, Tiferet, Malkhut.

Ish ("Man"). Tiferet inclusive of Keter, Ḥokhmah, and Binah.

Akhatriel (an angel). There are those who explain it [with reference] to Malkhut. It seems to me [to refer] to Creation.

El ("To"). This is a root word, as in *I will tell of* [el] *the decree* (Ps. 2:7), which is not holy. In the male world.

Eleh ("These"). They are the three Patriarchs[3] or the "Outside" ones, according to context.

El ("God"). Holy. It will be found in Keter and in Ḥesed and in Malkhut and in Yesod.

Eloha ("Deity"). *alef, lamed* [=] Ḥesed; *vav, heh* [=] Tiferet and Malkhut.

Eli ("My God"). Binah inclusive of the three first [sefirot].

Elisheva (feminine name). Malkhut deriving sustenance from the seven qualities.

Aluf ("Chief"). Tiferet.

Elokenu she-ba-Shamayim ("Our God in Heaven"). Binah.

Elokim Ḥayyim ("Living God"). Binah and Malkhut.

Elokekha ("Your God"). Binah and Malkhut.

Em ("Mother"). Binah and Malkhut.

Amah ("Cubit"). Tiferet inclusive of six *tefaḥim*,[4], six sefirot.

3. The sefirah Gedulah is associated with Abraham, Gevurah with Isaac, and Tiferet with Jacob.

4. The *tefaḥ* is a unit of measure.

Amen ("Amen"). Yesod uniting Tiferet and Malkhut and inclusive of the ten [sefirot].

Emon ("Hidden"). Keter, Tiferet, Yesod, Binah. [Cf.] the beginning of Bereshit Rabbah.[5]

Emunah ("Faith"). Binah from the side of Ḥesed; Malkhut from the side of Yesod.

Omenet ("Nursemaid"). Binah in relation to Tiferet.

Amoraim (sages of the Gemara). Gedulah, Gevurah, Tiferet.

Imrat ("The word of") Malkhut. The "word" is in Malkhut from the side of its being above.

Emesh ("Yesterday Evening"). They are Keter, Ḥokhmah, Binah.

Emet ("Truth"). Tiferet, sometimes inclusive of Tiferet, Malkhut, Yesod.

Ana ("Please"). Keter, Binah, Ḥokhmah.

Anaḥa ("Tribulation"). From the side of Tiferet.

Ani ("I"). Malkhut, Binah.

Aniyah ("Ship"). The powers of Malkhut are [as a] ship on the sea. [47a]

Anokhi ("I"). Binah and Malkhut.

Anfei Ravrevei ("Great Branches"). Gedulah and Gevurah or the high cherubs.

Anfei Zutrei ("Lesser Branches"). Neẓaḥ, Hod or the lower cherubs.

Istumkhah ("Stomach"). Malkhut.

5. The verse from Prov. 8:30 containing this word begins the first section of Bereshit Rabbah (1:1).

Ispaklariah ha-Me'irah ("Shining Mirror"). Tiferet.

[Ispaklariah] she-eina Me'irah ("The Mirror That Does Not Shine"). Malkhut and also Neẓaḥ, Hod. Also, Malkhut from the side of Gevurah.

Afisat ha-Ra'ayon ("Nullification of the Mind"). Keter.

Afikei Mayim ("Streams of Water"). Neẓaḥ, Hod.

Afelah ("Darkness"). Gevurah.

Efroaḥ ("Fledgling"). Tiferet and Yesod.

Apirion ("Palanquin"). Malkhut inclusive of the ten [sefirot].

Aparsimon ("Persimmon"). Binah inclusive of the six "directions" covering four.

Eẓbaot ("Fingers"). Ten [indicate] the ten sefirot; five constitute Gedulah, Gevurah, Tiferet, Neẓaḥ, Hod.

Argaman ("Purple"). Tiferet, Gedulah, Gevurah, Malkhut.

Arokh ("Long"). Tiferet.

Aron ("Ark"). Malkhut.

Arzei Levanon ("Cedars of Lebanon"). The existence of the sefirot within Keter.

Aryeh ("Lion"). Ḥesed.

Erekh 'Apayim ("Slow to Anger"). Tiferet from the aspect of Keter or Keter itself.

Armonot ("Palaces"). Neẓaḥ and Hod constitute the "palaces" for Malkhut.

Ereẓ ("Earth"). Malkhut. It is all according to the accompanying name.

Esh ("Fire"). Gevurah.

Ishah ("Woman"). Malkhut. The same for *Isheh* ("Fire Offering").

Ashmorot ("Watches"). Neẓaḥ, Hod.

Ashishot ("Cake"). The union brought about by white fire and red fire; or Gedulah, Gevurah, Tiferet.

Eshkolot ("Bunches of Grapes"). Neẓaḥ, Hod.

Osher ("Happiness"). Binah or Tiferet.

Asherah ("Grove"). Malkhut when it derives sustenance from Tiferet.

'Et (Particle designating direct object). Malkhut which is crowned from *alef* to *tav*.

'At ("You" [fem.]). Malkhut.

'Atah ("You" [masc.]). Tiferet and in Ḥesed and Malkhut and in Ḥokhmah and in Binah.

Etanim ("Mighty Ones"). Neẓaḥ, Hod, Yesod. [47b]

Etrog ("Citron"). Malkhut.

Letter *Bet*

Be'er ("Well"). Malkhut.

Beged (Garment"). Malkhut.

Bohu ("Void"). Gedulah.

Boaz. Hod.

Bakar ("Cattle"). Ḥesed or Yesod.

Betten ("Belly"). Binah.

Binah is so called when she unites with Ḥokhmah.

Bayit ("House"). Malkhut and Binah.

Beyt Din ("House of Judgment, Court"). Malkhut when she is [part of] three [sefirot] with Gedulah, Gevurah, and Tiferet.

Bekhor ("Firstborn"). Keter and Ḥokhmah and Tiferet.

Bamot ("High Places"). Gedulah, Gevurah, Tiferet.

Ben ("Son"). Tiferet.

Benot Yerushalayim ("Daughters of Jerusalem"). The souls or the twelve cattle under the sea.

Bar ("Outside"). The Righteous [Yesod] is exiled from his place to the "Outside."

Beẓah ("Egg"). Malkhut. There are those who have explained that the great measure [Egg][6] refers to the upper *yod*, Ḥokhmah, and the smaller measure of an Olive refers to the lower *yod*, Malkhut.

Barad ("Hail"). Ḥesed, and I am close to saying that it is Gevurah-within-Ḥesed.

6. The *beẓah* is a measure of bulk. It is a larger unit than the *zayit*.

Barukh ("Blessed"). Keter or the ten sefirot together or Yesod or Malkhut.

Barzel ("Iron"). Malkhut or Tiferet.

Beriḥim ("Bars"). Five sefirot: Ḥesed, Paḥad [Gevurah], Tiferet, Neẓaḥ, Hod.

Beriaḥ Tikhon ("The Middle Bar"). Tiferet.

Baraita[7] ("Outside Tradition"). Malkhut in exile and wandering.

Berit ("Covenant"). Tiferet or Malkhut or Yesod.

Berekhah ("Pool"). Malkhut.

Berakhah ("Blessing"). Malkhut from the side of Ḥesed.

Berakim ("Thunders") from the side of Yesod.

Basar ("Flesh"). Malkhut.

Bat (Daughter"). Malkhut.

Batei Gavaei ("Innermost Houses"). The three first [sefirot].

Bataei Baraei ("Outermost Houses"). The seven [lower] qualities.

7. A baraita is a Tannaitic tradition which does not appear in the Mishnah.

Letter *Gimel*

Geulah ("Redemption"). Binah or Yesod; Neẓaḥ, Hod, Yesod, Malkhut [are] the four "redemptions."[8] [48a]

Geon ("Pride"). According to the continuation that is consequent on the [connection with the sefirotic] quality, she [Malkhut] is "prideful".

Geut ha-Yam ("Tide"). Thread of Ḥesed upon Malkhut.

Gavoha ("Height"). Essentially [referring] to Eyn Sof; sometimes to the rest of the qualities, as in *for one higher than the high watches* (Eccles. 5:7). In any event, the "Height" is only [evident] from the addition of his emanation.

Gevul ("Border"). Malkhut.

Gevurah ("Bravery"). The quality of harsh judgment; sometimes [refers to] Binah.

Gevir ("Lord"). Malkhut.

Geva'ot ("Hills"). Binah and Malkhut.

Gag ha-Ḥofeh ("Covering Roof"). Keter.

Gad. Malkhut.

Gedulah ("Greatness"). Ḥesed.

Geviyah ("Body"). Yesod and Tiferet.

Gulgolet ("Skull"). The three first [sefirot].

Gulot ha-Kotarot ("Bowls of the Capitals" [I Kings 7:41]). Ḥesed and Gevurah; Yesod is the "Golden Bowl" (Eccles. 12:6).

8. This refers to the four verbs signifying redemption in Exod. 6:6: "I will bring you out . . . I will deliver you . . . I will redeem you . . . I will take you."

Gid ha-Nasheh ("Sciatic Nerve"). Yesod with Malkhut.

Gehinnom ("Gehenna"). Gevurah from the side of the "Outside" ones.

Ge Ḥizzayon ("Valley of Vision" [Isa. 22:4]). Malkhut.

Gal Na'ul ("A Spring Shut Up" [Song of Songs 4:12]). Malkhut.

Galgalei ha-Merkavah ("Wheels of the Chariot"). Neẓaḥ and Hod.

Galim ("Heaps"). Forces in Malkhut and Binah.

Gamal ("Camel"). The *Kelipah*.

Gemilut Ḥasadim ("Acts of Lovingkindness").] The overflow of Ḥesed.

Gan ("Garden"). Binah and Malkhut.

Gefen ("Vine"). Malkhut.

Ger ("Stranger"). Tiferet when it is out of its place.

Letter *Daled*

Dibbur ("Speech"). Malkhut.

Davar ("Word"). Malkhut.

Devash ("Honey"). From the side of Gevurah.

Du Parẓufin ("Dual Figure"). Tiferet and Malkhut.

Dod Ne'eman ("Faithful Love"). Yesod.

David. Malkhut.

Dor ("Generation"). Yesod and Tiferet; or Binah and Malkhut. This is [what is meant by the expression] *to all generations* (Exod. 3:15).

Dyo ("Ink"). In Binah, which gives the *vav* in the [divine] Name its due nourishment. With it is written the Torah scroll in the mystery of "black fire on top of white fire."[9] [48b]

Dayyan ("Judge"). Gevurah or Tiferet from the side of Malkhut.

Din Torah ("Judgment of the Torah"). True judgment; Malkhut.

Dakh ("Oppressed"). Yesod.

Dakhim ("Oppressed" [pl.]). Malkhut from the side of Yesod.

Dal ("Poor"). Yesod.

Dam ("Blood"). The closing of the emanation in Binah so that it does not come to Malkhut. Therefore it comes as *she has surely drawn* (Exod. 2:19), and with her the *mem* is closed.

Dimayon ("Imagination"). Malkhut.

Dema'ot ("Tears"). Gevurah, Hod.

Da'at ("Knowledge"). Tiferet or Yesod in the delicate aspect.

9. Yerushalmi, Shekalim 6:1.

Dar ("Dwells"). Malkhut or Binah.

Deror ("Freedom"). Binah.

Darom ("South"). Ḥesed.

Derakhim ("Paths"). The channels of the emanation from the three "patriarchs" to Malkhut.

Letter *Heh*

Heh (the letter). When it comes at the beginning of a word, it hints at Binah, and when it comes at the end of a word the hint is to Malkhut.

Hevel ("Vanity"). Seven "Vanities" are the seven [lower sefirotic] qualities.

Haggadah ("Recital"). From the side of Ḥokhmah.

Hadom ("Footstool"). Malkhut.

Hadas ("Myrtle"). The three "patriarchs." Malkhut [is called] *Hadassah.*[10]

Hadar ("Glory"). In Tiferet or Neẓaḥ.

Hu ("He"). In Keter or in Binah or in Tiferet or in Malkhut.

Hod ("Majesty"). It is so called when it is held by Gevurah and Binah.

Havah ("To Exist"). Hints at the upper *heh*, the lower *heh*, and the *vav* in the middle.[11]

Havi ("Existence"). Tiferet removes itself with the blessings to Binah.

Hi ("She"). Malkhut.

Heikhal ("Palace"). Malkhut.

Halakhah ("Law"). Malkhut.

10. Hadassah was Esther's name. Cf. Esther 2:7.

11. This is a reference to the three sefirot, Gedulah, Gevurah, and Tiferet. Cf. sec. 6, chap. 5, n. 29 above.

Hallel (Psalms of Praise). Malkhut when it is not completed.[12] Completed [it refers] to the side of Binah or to Binah herself.

Halleluyah ("Praise the Lord"). Malkhut from the side of Tiferet.

Hinneni ("Here am I"). Malkhut.

Har ("Mountain"). Malkhut. All is in accordance with the [divine] Name which accompanies [it].

Hatkafah ("Attack"). Malkhut from the side of Ḥesed.

12. Hallel is a series of psalms of praise recited in the synagogue on various holidays. On some of them, not all the psalms are recited and the Hallel is considered "incomplete."

Letter *Vav*

Vav (the letter). At the beginning of a word it indicates Tiferet. Thus *V'ani* ("And I") [indicates] Tiferet and Malkhut.

Vh. He and His court.

Vhu. Tiferet.

Vay ("Woe"). Tiferet removing the blessings from Yesod to him.

Vayehi ("And it came to pass"). From the side of Gevurah.

Vilon ("Curtain"). Malkhut.

Va'ad ("Assembly"). Binah, for she assembles the sefirot.

Veset ("Period"). The powers under Malkhut which are called *Ishim*.[13]

13. Ishim is the lowest order of angels. Cf. Maimonides, *Mishneh Torah* Hilkhot Yesodei ha-Torah 2:7.

Letter *Zayin*

Zot ("This" [fem.]). Malkhut.

Zevul ("Celestial Abode"). Binah.

Zeh ("This" [masc.]). Tiferet, Yesod.

Zahav ("Gold"). Binah or Gevurah.

Zayit ("Olive"). Malkhut. Sometimes the seven [lower sefirotic] qualities are all [called] "olives."

Zakhor ("Remember"). Tiferet.

Zekhirah ("Remembrance"). From the side of Yesod.

Zekhut ("Merit"). Gevurah or Ḥesed and the essence of *y[od].*

Za'akah ("Cry"). Binah.

Zekifah ("Standing Upright"). From the side of Tiferet.

Zaken ("Old Man"). Keter.

Zeraḥ ("Brightness"). Tiferet.

Zero'ot ("Limbs"). Ḥesed, Gevurah.

Zeret ("Span"). Gevurah, Malkhut with her maidens.

Letter *Ḥet*

Ḥavush ("Put On" [the Head]). Tiferet.

Ḥayon ("Secret Place"). Keter or the three first [sefirot].

Ḥevel ("Rope"). Tiferet.

Ḥavit ("Barrel"). Binah.

Ḥavaẓelet ("Lily"). Malkhut.

Ḥag ("Holiday"). Malkhut.

Ḥadarim ("Rooms"). Seven [lower sefirotic] qualities hidden within Binah.

Ḥadash ("New"). In Malkhut which renews [herself].

Ḥazeh ("Breast"). Binah

Ḥozeh ("Seer"). Tiferet.

Ḥut ha-Shidra ("Spinal Cord"). The middle line. [49b]

Ḥotam ("Nose"). Tiferet.

Ḥulia ("Link"). Shekhinah[14] with the three "Patriarchs."

Ḥom ha-Yom ("Heat of the Day"). The brightness of Ḥesed.

Ḥomah ("Wall"). Malkhut.

Ḥosen ("Riches"). Tiferet.

Ḥuppah ("Canopy"). Keter. Its roof is Ḥokhmah; its walls are Binah; its doors are Gedulah and Gevurah; its pillars are Neẓaḥ and Hod; underneath it are the bridegroom, the bride, and the attendant: Tiferet and Malkhut and Yesod.

14. I.e., Malkhut.

Ḥokkekei Yisrael ("Legislators of Israel"). "Father" and "Mother"[15] from the emanators of Tiferet.

Ḥotam ("Seal"). Binah, Ḥokhmah, Tiferet.

Ḥazu ("Foretelling"). Of the night; Gabriel.

Ḥizzuk ("Strengthening"). Tiferet with Malkhut.

Ḥazhazit ("Lichen"?). Tiferet removed in Malkhut.

Ḥitah ("Wheat"). Malkhut.

Ḥet ("Sin"). Male Serpent.[16]

Ḥattat ("Sin"). Female, Woman of Whoredom.[17]

Ḥai ("Living"). Yesod.

Ḥayyah ("Living" [fem.]). Malkhut.

Ḥayyei ha-Melekh ("Life of the King"). Ḥokhmah and Binah.

Ḥayyim ("Life"). The first three [sefirot].

Ḥiyekh ("Smile"). Ḥokhmah.

Ḥeli ("My Host"). Eyn Sof.

Ḥayil ("Virtue"). Ḥokhmah which is *yod.*

Ḥerut ("Freedom"). Binah.

Ḥorin ("Free"). Ḥokhmah and Binah.

Ḥalav ("Milk"). The abundance which emanates from Keter through Ḥokhmah to Binah.

Ḥallah ("Consecrated Dough"). Malkhut.

15. Ḥokhmah and Binah.

16. Samael, the evil counterpart, on the "Other Side," to the sefirah Tiferet. Cf. Zohar I, 147a-148b.

17. Lilith, Samael's consort.

Ḥalom ("Dream"). Malkhut from her own side.

Ḥalon ("Window"). Tiferet.

Ḥalaẓaim ("Loins"). The union of Tiferet with Malkhut between Neẓah and Hod.

Ḥam ("Warm"). From the side of Gevurah.

Ḥemdat Yamim ("Love of Life"). She is the Shekhinah.

Ḥammah ("Sun"). Tiferet.

Ḥamishah ("Five"). The hint is to Tiferet or Malkhut.

Ḥanun ("Merciful"). In Ḥesed and the essence in Binah.

Ḥessed ("Kindness"). In its place and in Keter and in Neẓah and in Hod. They are: Keter [is] the upper Ḥesed. Neẓaḥ, Hod [are] "The Kindnesses of David."[18]

Ḥassid ("Pious"). Ḥokhmah in Ḥesed.

Ḥassidah ("Stork"). Binah over Ḥesed or Malkhut from the side of Ḥesed. [50a]

Ḥafeẓ ("Possession"). Malkhut from the side of Tiferet in the emanation of Keter.

Ḥofshi ("Free"). Binah.

Ḥaẓẓot Laylah ("Midnight"). Malkhut from the side of Mercy.

Ḥaẓẓi ("Half"). From the side of Malkhut which is a portion of Matzah.[19]

Ḥizzim ("Arrows"). From the side of Yesod.

18. Cf. Isa. 55:3.

19. This is a reference to the ceremonial breaking of a matzah at the Passover Seder.

Ḥaẓẓoẓrot Kessef ("Silver Trumpets"). Neẓaḥ and Hod from the side of Ḥesed.

Ḥaẓerot Ha[Shem] ("Courts of the Lord"). The seven [lower sefirotic] qualities.

Ḥok ("Law"). Yesod.

Ḥukkah ("Decree"). Malkhut.

Ḥukkot ("Laws"). The powers of Malkhut below.

Ḥeker ("Inquiry"). Malkhut.

Ḥerev ("Sword"). Gevurah and essentially all YDVH or Malkhut.

Ḥoshekh ("Darkness"). In Malkhut and in Gevurah and in Keter and in the "Outside."

Ḥashmal ("Electrum"). Neẓaḥ, Hod; the mystery of [the Name] YAHDVNHY.

Ḥeshkehem ("Their Desire"). Neẓaḥ, Hod.

Ḥatan ("Bridegroom"). Tiferet.

Letter *Tet*

Tabur ("Navel"). Malkhut from the side of Binah.

Taba'at ("Ring"). Malkhut [from the side] of Ḥokhmah. The essential secret of the closed *mem* [Isa. 9:6]; Binah in Ḥokhmah.

Taharah ("Purification") from the side of Ḥesed or from the side of Gevurah.

Tov ("Good" [masc.]). In Ḥesed or in Keter or in Yesod.

Tovah ("Good" [fem.]). Malkhut.

Tuv Yerushalayim ("The Good of Jerusalem" [Ps. 128:5]). Concerning Malkhut from Tiferet.

Taḥol ("Spleen"). "Outside."

Taḥanot ("Stations"). Neẓaḥ and Hod, or the [angelic] powers under Malkhut called *Ishim*.

Tal ("Dew"). In Tiferet the combination of *yod, heh, vav.*

Tallit ("Garment, Prayer Garment"). Moon; Tiferet from the side of Ḥesed. It is appropriate in many places.

Tene ("Basket"). Malkhut.

Tipah ("Drop"). Malkhut.

Tefaḥ ("Span"). Malkhut from the side of the five sefirot.

[50b]

Letter *Yod*

Y'or ("Nile"). Yesod.

Yabbok (Jabbok). Gedulah, Gevurah, Tiferet; three paths, the path of Judgment, the path of Mercy, the path of Lovingkindness.

Yabashah ("Dry Land"). Malkhut.

Yad ("Hand"). Malkhut or Binah; from the side of Gevurah.

Yad ha-Ḥazakah ("Strong Hand"). From the side of Tiferet.

Yad Ramah ("Upraised Hand"). From the side of Ḥesed.

Yad ha-Gedolah ("Great Hand"). Knowledge, signifying the union of male and female.

Yehi ("It Will Be"). Tiferet.

Yovel ("Jubilee"). Binah.

Yom ("Day"). Tiferet and sometimes in its place others like Ḥesed and Binah according to the context.

Yomam ("Daily"). Ḥesed.

Yonah ("Dove"). Malkhut.

Yosef (Joseph). Yesod.

Yo'eẓ ("Advisor"). Binah.

Yoẓer Bereshit ("Creator"). Ḥokhmah.

Yoteret ha-Kaved ("Membrane on the Liver"). The woman of harlotry.

Yiḥud ("Union"). Refers to Tiferet and Malkhut, and all the sefirot accompany them.

Yakhin ("Pillar"). Neẓaḥ.

Yeladim ("Children"). Neẓaḥ and Hod.

Yam ("Seal"). Binah or Ḥokhmah.

Yamim ("Days"). The seven [lower] sefirot. Previously in *arikh anpin.*[20]

Yamin ("Right"). Ḥesed, and sometimes Neẓaḥ or Ḥokhmah.

Ya'akov (Jacob). Malkhut filled with [flow from] Tiferet.

Yefe Nof ("Beauteous View"). Tiferet or Yesod.

Yefe Enayim ("Beautiful to the Eyes"). Malkhut from the side where they wash with milk.

Yiẓḥak (Isaac). Gevurah.

Yir'eh ("He Will See"). Gevurah or Binah or Malkhut.

Yarum ("He Will Raise Up"). Binah from the side of Ḥokhmah.

Yerushalayim (Jerusalem). Malkhut.

Yare'aḥ ("Moon"). Malkhut.

Yeriah ("Curtain"). Tiferet.

Yarketey Ẓafon ("Furthest Place in the North"). Neẓaḥ and Hod from the side of Gevurah.

Yesh ("Exists"). Ḥokhmah in partnership with Binah.

Yeshuah ("Salvation"). From the side of Ḥesed.

Yeshurun (Jeshurun). Tiferet, inclusive of Right and Left.

[51a]

Yeshivah shel Ma'alah ("Court on High"). Binah.

20. An aspect of the sefirah Keter.

Yashar ("Upright"). Malkhut together with Tiferet.

Yeshenei Afar ("Those Who Sleep in the Dust"). The three "Patriarchs" in Malkhut.

Yisrael (Israel). Tiferet as decisive force between Ḥokhmah and Binah.

Letter *Kaf*

Kabed ("Liver"). The male [partner] of the *kelipah.* [Cf.] *Yoteret ha-Kaved*—Lilith.

Kavod ("Glory"). The Shekhinah joined with Yesod.

Kevodi ("My Glory"). Binah and all is in the mystery of the thirty-two paths.[21]

Kevosh ("Conquer"). Tiferet.

Kabir ("Mighty"). Gevurah.

Kevar (name of river [see. Ezek. 1:2]). Keter, Binah, Reshit [= Ḥokhmah].

Kevasim ("Sheep"). The seven [lower] sefirot either from the side of Binah or of Ḥesed.

Kivshan ("Furnace"). Malkhut which is covering and "cooking" the seed.

Kad ("Pitcher"). Yesod.

Kada ("Her Pitcher"). Malkhut.

Koh ("Thus"). Malkhut or Binah.

Kohen ("Priest"). Ḥesed.

Kova Yeshuah ("Hat of Salvation"). Eyn Sof or Tiferet or Malkhut.

Kos Shel Berakhah ("Goblet of Benediction"). Malkhut from the side of her hosts.

Kos Yeshuot ("Goblet of Salvation"). [Malkhut] in her joining with the salvations.

21. Cf. *Sefer Yeẓirah* 1:1.

Kotel ("Wall"). Tiferet with Malkhut at the hand of Yesod.

Kiyor ve-Kano ("Basin and Its Pedestal"). Neẓaḥ and Hod.

Koaḥ ("Strength"). Binah from the side of Ḥokhmah.

Ki, Kol ("That, All"). Yesod.

Kallah ("Bride"). Malkhut. All is from the side of Binah and from the side of Ḥesed.

Kelayot ("Kidneys"). Neẓaḥ and Hod.

Kinnor ("Harp"). Malkhut.

Kenesset Yisrael ("Communion of Israel"). Malkhut.

Kanaim ("Submissions"). The name YHVD.

Kanfei ha-Ain ("The Wings of the Eye"). Neẓaḥ and Hod.

Kissei Din ("Seat of Judgment"). Malkhut.

Kissei Raḥamim ("Seat of Mercy"). Tiferet.

Kes ("Seat"). Malkhut, [as in] *for the hand on the seat of God* (Exod. 17:16).

Kessef ("Silver"). Ḥesed.

Kaf Zekhut ("Merit"). Ḥesed.

Kaf Ḥovah ("Demerit"). Gevurah.

Kippurim ("Atonement"). Binah. [51b]

Kaporet ("Covering"). Yesod.

Kapot ("Handles"). Yesod.

Keruvim ("Cherubs"). Metatron, Sandalfon; or Neẓaḥ and Hod, or Tiferet and Malkhut.

Kerem ("Vineyard"). Malkhut.

Keriah ("Bowing"). Neẓaḥ and Hod or the Righteous [Yesod].

Ketuvim ("Writings"). Malkhut or Ḥesed and Gevurah.

Katit ("Squeezed"). Yesod.

Katef Yamin ("Right Shoulder"). Binah.

Katef Smol ("Left Shoulder"). Malkhut.

Letter *Lamed*

Lev ("heart"). Malkhut.

Levonah ("Frankincense"). Ḥokhmah or Hod.

Levanah ("White"). The unclean side.

Levanah ("Moon"). Malkhut.

Levanon ("Lebanon"). Keter.

Lahav ("Flame"). Malkhut.

Lahat ha-Ḥerev ("The Flashing Blade" [Gen. 3:24]). Malkhut from the side of Metatron.

Luḥot ("Tablets"). Neẓaḥ and Hod.

Levi (Levi [tribe]). Gevurah.

Livyatan (Leviathan). Tiferet, Yesod.

Leḥem ("Bread"). Malkhut.

Leḥem ha-Panim ("Showbread"). Yesod.

Lot ("Charm"). The strap of evil.

Li ("Mine"). Binah.

Layish, *Laysha* ("Lion, Lioness"). Tiferet and Malkhut.

Lekha ("Come"). Binah or Malkhut.

Limmudei ha-Shem ("Learned of the Lord"). Neẓaḥ and Hod.

Lifnei or *Lifanai* ("Before" or "Before Me"). Malkhut.

Lashon ("Tongue"). Binah or Yesod or Malkhut.

Lishkat ha-Gazit ("Chamber of Hewn Stones," in the Temple). Malkhut.

Letter *Mem*

Me'od ("Greatly"). Tiferet from the side of Gevurah.

Me'or Gadol ("The Greater Light"; the sun). Tiferet.

Me'or Katan ("The Lesser Light"; the moon). Malkhut.

Ma'akhal ("Food"). The emanation.

Me'orot ("Lights"). [May refer to] the side of holiness or [that of] impurity.

Mabua ("Spring"). Keter.

Migdal ("Tower"). Binah or Malkhut or Keter.

Magen ("Shield"). Malkhut. [52a]

Madon ("Quarrel"). Judgment [Din]. Thus also *midyan* ("quarrel").

Middat Yom ("Quality of Day"). Tiferet.

Middat Laylah ("Quality of Night"). Malkhut.

Middat ha-Din ha-Kasha ("The Harsh Quality of Judgment"). Gevurah.

Middat ha-Din ha-Rafah ("The Mild Quality of Judgment"). Malkhut.

Mah ("What"). Ḥokhmah or Tiferet or Malkhut.

Moaḥ ("Brain"). Ḥokhmah.

Mot ("Staff"). Tiferet with Yesod.

Mosdei Ereẓ ("Foundations of the Land"). The Righteous [Yesod] and Righteousness.

Musaf ("Additional" [Service]). Yesod.

Mo'ed ("Appointed Time"). The six "directions".[22]

22. The six "directions" are the six sefirot from Gedulah to Yesod.

Muflah ("Wondrous"). Keter.

Mar ("Bitter"). Keter.

Mor ("Myrrh"). Ḥesed.

Moshiah ("Savior"). Tiferet.

Moshel ("Ruler"). Tiferet from the side of Yesod.

Mavet (Death"). The evil.

Mizbe'aḥ Pnimi (The Inner Altar). Binah.

Mizbe'aḥ ha-ḥiẓẓon ("The Outer Altar"). Malkhut.

Mezuzot ("Doorposts"). Neẓaḥ and Hod.

Mezuzah ("Doorpost"). Malkhut from the side of Tiferet.

Mazon ("Food"). Ḥesed.

Mazal ("Fortune"). Keter.

Mizmor ("Song"). Ḥesed, Malkhut.

Mizraḥ ("East"). Ḥokhmah, Binah, Tiferet.

Maḥazeh ("Vision"). Malkhut alone.

Maḥazit ha-Shekel ("Half-Shekel"). Tiferet.

Maḥshavah ("Thought"). Eyn Sof, Keter, Ḥokhmah, Binah.

Maḥshof ha-Lavan ("The White Exposed Place" [Gen. 30:37]). Keter or Tiferet.

Mattah ("Below"). Malkhut.

Matteh ("Staff"). Tiferet or Binah.

Matarah ("Goal"). Malkhut.

Matronah ("Lady"). [The division of] Creation, or Malkhut.

Metatron (angel). Shekhinah.

Mi ("Who"). Binah.

Mayim ("Water"). Ḥesed.

Milah ("Circumcision"). Yesod.

Makhon (name of sixth heaven). Malkhut.

Mekhuseh ("Covered"). Keter.

Makhpelah ("Double"). Malkhut or Binah.

Makhria ("Arbitrator"). Tiferet or the Righteous [Yesod].

Mikhtam ("Poem"). Tiferet and Yesod.

Malei ("Full"). Emanation.

Malakh ("Angel"). Malkhut. [Malkhut is also referred to by the terms] *melukhah* ("kingdom") and *malon* ("dwelling place").

Melaḥ. ("Salt"). Yesod.

Melekh ("King"). Tiferet. [52b]

Melekh Shelomoh ("King Solomon"). Tiferet or Binah or Ḥokhmah.

Malki Ẓedek (Melchizedek). Malkhut.

Mamlekhet Kohanim ("Kingdom of Priests" [Exod. 19:6]). Malkhut with Tiferet.

Menuḥah ("Rest"). Binah.

Menorah ("Lamp). Shekhinah, [which is also referred to by the words] *minḥah* ("gift") and *mispar* ("number").

Maon ("Dwelling"). Keter, Ḥokhmah, Malkhut.

Ma'ayan ("Spring"). The three first [sefirot] and the three last [sefirot].

Ma'ayanei ha-Yeshuah ("Wells of Salvation"). Ḥokhmah and Binah, Ḥesed and Gevurah.

Me'al ha-Shamayim ("Above the Heavens"). Binah.

Ma'amakim ("Depths"). Ḥokhmah, Keter.

Ma'arav ("West"). Malkhut.

Ma'arakhah ("Army"). Binah or Malkhut. [These are also referred to by the term] *ma'aseh* ("deed").

Ma'aseh Merkavah ("Account of the Chariot"). Metatron.

Ma'aseh Bereshit ("Account of Creation"). Malkhut [which is also referred to by the term] *ma'aser* ("tithe").

Maẓevah ("Pillar"). Malkhut with Tiferet.

Maẓah ("Unleavened Bread"). Malkhut.

Miẓvah ("Commandment"). Malkhut.

Miẓuveh ("One Who Is Commanded"). Tiferet and Yesod.

Meẓulot Yam ("Depths of the Sea"). *Kelipah*.

Mikdash ("Sanctuary"). Tiferet and Yesod.

Mikveh ("Source of Water"). Malkhut and Tiferet.

Makom ("Place"). Tiferet.

Makor ("Source"). Keter.

Makel ("Staff"). Tiferet.

Maklot ("Staffs"). The forces of Judgment.

Mikneh ("Cattle"). From the side of Malkhut.

Mikraei Kodesh ("Holy Convocations"). The three "patriarchs."

Mar'eh ("Vision"). Malkhut, Binah.

Marah ("Bitter"). Wicked Lilith.

Merkavah ("Chariot"). Any [group of] four sefirot is called *merkavah*.

Mishbezot ("Setting" [of gems]). Neẓaḥ and Hod.

Mesos ("Joy"). Tiferet.

Mashkon ("Pledge"). Malkhut.

Maskil ("Enlightened"). Yesod, Binah.

Mishkan ("Tabernacle"). Binah, Malkhut.

Mishalem Gemul ("Payer of Recompense"). Fear.

Mishnah (Mishnah). Malkhut.

Mishpat ("Judgment"). Tiferet.

Mashkof ("Lintel"). Yesod.

Matok ("Sweet"). Malkhut from the side of Gevuraḥ.

Mattan Torah ("Giving of the Torah"). Binah.

Mattanah Tovah ("Goodly Gift"). Malkhut. [53a]

Motnayim ("Thighs"). Neẓaḥ, Hod.

Letter *Nun*

Na'ah ("Comely"). Malkhut.

Ne'eman ("Faithful"). Yesod.

Nevuah ("Prophecy"). Malkhut.

Nevi'im ("Prophets"). Neẓaḥ and Hod.

Negev ("South"). Ḥesed from the side of Gevurah.

Niggun ("Tune"). Binah.

Nega ("Plague"). *Kelipah.*

Nedivim ("Princes"). Three patriarchs.

Neder ("Vow"). Binah.

Nahar ("River"). Ḥokhmah, Binah, Tiferet, Yesod.

Nogah ("Brightness"). Neẓaḥ.

Naveh ("Pasture"). Malkhut.

Nozlim ("Flow"). Five sefirot.

No'am ("Pleasantness"). The overflow of Malkhut.

Noẓer ("Guard"). Tiferet, [which is also referred to by the term] *nora* ("awesome").

Nose' Avon ("Forgiving Sin"). Yesod.

Noaḥ (Noah). Yesod.

Niḥoaḥ ("Savory"). Emanation.

Naḥal ("Stream"). Binah, Yesod.

Naḥalah ("Inheritance"). Binah.

Nimah ("Thread"). Yesod, [which is also referred to by the term] *nes* ("miracle").

Na'al ("Shoe") and *Na'ar* ("Lad"). Metatron.

Nefesh ("Soul"). Malkhut.

Niẓav ("Standing"). The [sefirotic] unity above Yesod.

Niẓanim ("Buds"). Three patriarchs.

Nakam ("Revenge"). Malkhut.

Ner ("Candle"). Malkhut.

Nerd ("Spikenard"). Yesod.

Neshikah ("Kiss"). The Unity.

Nissa ("Uplifted"). Tiferet, Keter.

Neshamah ("Soul"). Binah.

Nesher ("Eagle"). Malkhut.

Letter *Samekh*

Sabba de-Sabbin ("Oldest of the Old"). Ḥokhmah, Keter.

Savta ("Old Woman"). Binah.

Sibbat ha-Sibbot ("First Cause"). Keter.

Segulah ("Precious"). Malkhut.

Seder Zemanim ("Sequence of Time"). Tiferet and Malkhut.

Sod ("Secret"). The Righteous [Yesod].

Sukkah ("Booth"). Binah, Malkhut.

Sof ("End"). The Righteous [Yesod].

Soḥaret ("Onyx"). Ḥokhmah.

Siyyata ("Help"). Malkhut.

Sarkhah ("Adhesion"). *Kelipah.* [53b]

Sal ("Basket"). Malkhut.

Selah ("Selah"). Binah, Malkhut.

Seliḥah ("Forgiveness"). Tiferet.

Sullam ("Ladder"). The righteous [Yesod], Tiferet.

Sela' ("Rock"). Malkhut or Beriyah.

Solet ("Fine Flour"). Malkhut.

Sandal ("Sandal"). Refers to [the angel] Sandalphon.

Sanhedrin Gedolah ("The Great Sanhedrin"). Tiferet. *Ketanah* ("The Lesser [Sanhedrin]"). Malkhut.

Seudah ("Meal"). Binah, Malkhut.

Sa'ar ("Storm"). Judgment.

Sefirat ha-Omer ("Counting of the Omer"). Malkhut.

Sefer ("Book"). Tiferet, Malkhut, and the Righteous [Yesod].

Letter *'Ayin*

'Av ("Cloud"). Ḥesed.

'Ever ("Limb"). Malkhut or Metatron.

'Avodah ("Service"). Malkhut.

'Avodat ha-Levi'im ("The Service of the Levites"). Binah and Malkhut.

'Agulah ("Oval"). Binah.

'Egel ("Calf"). Gevurah, Malkhut.

'Ed ("Witness"). Binah, Malkhut, Yesod.

'Edah ("Congregation"). Malkhut.

'Edut ("Testimony"). The Unity.

'Eden (Eden). Keter.

'Ednah ("Pleasure"). Malkhut.

'Over 'al Pesha ("Overlooking Sin"). Tiferet, Yesod.

'Olah ("Burnt Offering"). Malkhut and Tiferet, near Binah.

'Olam ("World"). Tiferet, Binah, Malkhut

'Omek ("Depth"). All the sefirot.

'Omer ("Measure"). Binah.

'Of ("Bird"). Yesod, Metatron.

'Ofer ("Gazelle"). Tiferet.

'Oseh Pele ("Doing Wonders"). Tiferet.

'Eẓ ("Tree"). Gevurah.

'Oz ("Strength"). Tiferet.

'Ayin ("Eye"). Tiferet, Malkhut.

'Efatah ("Darkness"). Malkhut.

'Ir ("City"). Binah, Malkhut.

'Eruv ("Boundary"). Tiferet.

'Al ha-Shem ("On God"). The first three [sefirot].

'Al Shamayim ("Over the Heavens"). Gedulah, Gevurah.

'Al Kol Mayim ("Over All the Waters"). Binah.

'Elat ha-'Elot ("Source of Sources"). Keter.

'Amud ("Pillar"). Malkhut.

'Omer ("Sheaf"). Ḥesed.

'Anavim ("Grapes"). The six "directions."

'Oneg ("Delight"). Keter, Tiferet, Malkhut.

'Anavah ("Modesty"). Tiferet in Da'at. [54a]

'Ani ("Poor Man"). Yesod.

'Aniyah ("Poor Woman"). Malkhut.

'Anan ("Cloud"). Ḥesed.

'Anaf 'Ez̤ Avot ("Branch of the Leafy Tree" [Lev. 23:40]). The three "patriarchs."

'Afar ("Dust"). Malkhut.

'Ez̤ ("Tree"). Tiferet.

'Ez̤ev ("Sadness"). Judgment.

'Ez̤ah ("Advice"). Malkhut.

'Ez̤em ha-Shamayim ("The Essence of Heaven" [Exod. 24:10]). Malkhut.

'Az̤eret ("Assembly"). Malkhut.

'Ekev ("Heel"). Malkhut.

'Akedah ("Binding" [of Isaac]). Malkhut.

'Ikar ("Root"). Yesod.

'Akeret ("Barren Woman"). Malkhut.

'Erev ("Evening"). Gevurah, Hod.

'Aravot ("Clouds"). Tiferet or Yesod.

'Arvei Naḥal ("Willows of the Brook" [Lev. 23:40]). Neẓaḥ and Hod.

'Arvit (Evening prayer). Tiferet or Yesod.

'Arugah ("Flower Bed"). Malkhut.

'Arafel ("Thick Darkness"). Tiferet and Malkhut.

'Eres ("Bed"). Malkhut.

'Esev ("Grass"). Tiferet.

'Oseh Peri ("Fruit-bearing"). Tiferet.

'Ashan ("Smoke"). The awakening.

'Asiyyah ("Making"). Tiferet.

'Eser, 'Asor ("Ten, Tenth"). Malkhut.

'Issaron ("One Tenth"). All the sefirot in Malkhut.

'Et ("Time"). Malkhut.

'Atikah ("Ancient"). Keter, Ḥokhmah.

'Atar ("Entreaty"). Keter.

Letter *Peh*

Pe'er ("Glory"). Binah.

Peh ("Mouth"). Malkhut or Gedulah, Gevurah.

Poked Avod ("Who visits the sins" [Exod. 20:5]). Gevurah.

Peter Reḥem ("Firstborn"). Malkhut.

Pele ("Wonder"). Ḥokhmah.

Peleg ("Brook"). Binah, Malkhut.

Panim ("Face"). Tiferet.

Pesak ("Judgment"). Malkhut.

Pekudah ("Order"). Malkhut.

Pekudim ("Commandments"). Neẓaḥ and Hod.

Pekidah ("Visitation"). Malkhut.

Parah ("Calf"). Binah, Malkhut.

Perat ("Detail"). Tiferet.

Peri 'Etz ("Fruit of Tree"). Malkhut.

Periah ("Uncovering" [in the context of circumcision]). Yesod or Malkhut.

Parokhet ("Curtain"). Malkhut.

Parnas ("Chief"). Binah, Malkhut.

Peshuta ("Simple"). Ḥesed. [54b]

Petaḥ ("Gate"). Malkhut.

Letter *Ẓadi*

Ẓava ("Host"). Neẓaḥ and Hod.

Ẓevi ("Stag"). Yesod.

Ẓiviah ("Deer"). Malkhut.

Ẓaddik ("Righteous"). Yesod.

Ẓedek ("Righteousness"). Malkhut.

Ẓedakah ("Charity"). Binah, Tiferet, Malkhut.

Ẓavar ("Neck"). Tiferet.

Ẓur ("Rock"). Binah, Gevurah, Malkhut.

Ẓorekh ha-'Olam ("The Necessity of the World"). Malkhut.

Ẓurat Zakhar ("The Male Image"). Tiferet.

Ẓaḥẓaḥot ("Brightness"). Binah.

Ẓiyyon ("Zion"). Yesod, Malkhut.

Ẓayin ("Indication"). Binah.

Ẓiẓit ("Fringes"). Shekhinah.

Ẓikei Kederah ("Fluid Spices"). Malkhut.

Ẓelalai 'Erev ("Evening Shadows"). "Shadow of Death" (Ps. 23:4), *kelipah.*

Ẓela ("Rib"). Malkhut.

Ẓela ha-Mishkan ("Beam of the Tabernacle" [Exod. 26:26]). Metatron.

Ẓintarot ha-Zahav ("Dignitary," lit. "Golden Pipe"). Ḥokhmah, Binah.

Ẓe'akah ("Outcry"). Binah.

Ẓafon ("North"). Gevurah.

Ẓippor ("Bird"). Malkhut.

Ẓeror ha-Ḥayyim ("The Web of Life"). Binah, Tiferet, Malkhut.

Ẓerikha ("Needy"). Malkhut.

Letter *Kof*

Kabbalah ("Tradition"). Malkhut.

Kadosh ("Holy"). Keter, Tiferet, Yesod.

Kedushah (Holiness"). Malkhut.

Kodesh ("Holy"). From Binah on up.

Kav ("Line"). Tiferet.

Kal ("Swift"). Tiferet.

Kula ("Leniency" [in law]). Malkhut.

Kometz ("Handful"). Ḥokhmah.

Kayitz ("Summer"). Yesod.

Kor, Ḥom, Kayitz, Ḥoref ("Cold, heat, summer, winter" [Gen. 8:22]). The four "directions."

Kashiah ("Query"). Malkhut.

Ketoret ("Incense"). Like *kesher.*

Kibah ("Stomach"). *Kelipah.*

Kayyam ("Enduring"). Tiferet.

Kulmus ("Pen"). Tiferet.

Kan ("Nest"). Malkhut or Metatron.

Kaneh ("Reed"). Da'at.

Kefiẓah ("Jump"). Malkhut.

[55a]

Keẓ ("End"). Yesod.

Keravayim ("Innards"). The Ḥayot.[23]

23. The Ḥayyot are the highest of the ten orders of angels. Cf. n. 13 above.

Korban ("Sacrifice"). Malkhut.

Karov ("Close"). Yesod.

Kiriyah ("City"). Malkhut.

Keren ("Horn"). Tiferet and Malkhut.

Karsulim ("Ankles"). Neẓaḥ and Hod.

Karkevan ("Gizzard"). Like *iẓtumkah*.

Karka ("Land"). Malkhut.

Kesher ("Knot"). The three "patriarchs."

Keshet ("Rainbow"). Yesod.

Letter *Resh*

Ra'ayah ("Proof"). Ḥokhmah, Ḥesed, Binah, Gevurah.

Rosh ("Head"). Keter, Ḥesed, Tiferet, Yesod, Malkhut.

Reshit Ḥokhmah ("Beginning of Wisdom" [Ps. 111:10]). Malkhut.

Rav ("Great"). Ḥokhmah, Tiferet.

Ravua ("Square"). Binah.

Rabbim ("Many"). The three "patriarchs."

Rova ("Quarter"). Yesod.

Revi'it ("Fourth"). Malkhut.

Rivkah (Rebecca). Malkhut.

Raglayim ("Feet"). Malkhut.

Rehatim ("Rafters"). Neẓaḥ and Hod.

Rov ("Majority"). Yesod.

Ru'aḥ ("Spirit"). Tiferet, Malkhut.

Roḥav ("Width"). Malkhut.

Rokhev Shamayim ("Who rides upon the heavens" [Deut. 33:26]). Binah.

Rokhel ("Spice Merchant"). Yesod.

Rum ("Height"). Tiferet.

Rom ("Height"). Keter.

Rum Shamayim ("Height of Heaven"). Ḥokhmah.

Romakh ("Spear"). Tiferet.

Ro'eh ("Shepherd"). Tiferet.

Reḥovot ("Wide spaces"). Binah.

Raḥum ("Merciful"). Tiferet.

Raḥok ("Far"). Ḥokhmah.

Raḥel (Rachel). Malkhut.

Raḥamim ("Mercy"). Tiferet.

Riv ("Quarrel"). Malkhut.

Re'aḥ ("Scent"). Malkhut.

Ram ("High"). Binah.

Rimmonim ("Pomegranates"). Neẓaḥ and Hod.

Rinah ("Joy"). Yesod.

Rennanim ("Rejoicing"). Neẓaḥ and Hod, Ḥokhmah and Binah.

Re'emim ("Thunders"). Gevurah.

Ra'ash ("Noise"). Malkhut. [55b]

Raẓon ("Will"). Keter.

Rakia ("Firmament"). Tiferet, Binah.

Reshut ("Domain"). Malkhut.

Letter *Shin*

Sha'agah ("Roar"). Ḥesed.

She'elah ("Question"). Malkhut.

She'ar ("Remainder"). Malkhut.

Shavua ("Week"). Binah, Yesod, Malkhut.

Sheva ("Seven"). Yesod.

Sheva Shabbatot ("Seven Weeks"). Binah, also the Seven Days.

Sebakhot ("Lattice-work"). Ḥokhmah and Binah.

Shabbat ("Sabbath"). Malkhut.

Sadeh ("Field"). Malkhut.

Shidrat ha-Lulav ("Spine of the Lulav"). Yesod.

Seh ("Lamb"). Ḥesed.

Shoter ("Officer"). Tiferet.

Shokhen ("Dweller"). Tiferet.

Shulḥan ("Table"). Malkhut.

Sholet ("Ruler"). Tiferet.

Sha'avah ("Outcry"). Malkhut.

Shofet ("Judge"). Tiferet.

Shofar ("Ram's Horn"). Tiferet.

Shofar Gadol ("Great Shofar"). Binah.

Shevakim ("Marketplaces"). Neẓaḥ and Hod.

Shod ("Devastation"). Gevurah.

Shoshan ("Rose"). Neẓaḥ or Hod.

Shoshannah ("Rose"). Malkhut.

Sheḥakim ("Clouds"). Neẓaḥ and Hod.

Shaḥar ("Dawn"). Neẓaḥ.

Sitnah ("Enmity"). *Kelipah.*

Seva ("Old Age"). Keter.

Siaḥ ("Bush"). Yesod.

Shitah ("Acacia"). Malkhut.

Shir ("Song"). Ḥokhmah, Malkhut.

Shikhaḥa ("Forgotten Sheaf" [Deut. 24:19]). *Kelipah.*

Sekhel ("Intellect"). Keter, Ḥokhmah, Yesod, Malkhut.

Shokhen ("Dweller"). Yesod.

Sheleg ("Snow"). Tiferet and similarly *Shalhevet* ("Flame").

Shalom ("Peace"). Tiferet, Yesod.

Shalem ("Complete"). Malkhut.

Shelamim ("Peace Offerings"). Tiferet with Malkhut.

Sham ("There"), *Shem* ("Name"), *Shamor* ("Observe"), *Shemittah* ("Sabbatical Year"). Malkhut.

Simḥah ("Joy"). Binah.

Shamayim ("Heaven"). Tiferet.

Shamayimah ("Toward Heaven"), *Shemini* ("Eighth"). Malkhut.

Shemi'ah ("Hearing"). Gevurah. [56a]

Shemirah ("Guarding"). Malkhut.

Shemen ("Oil"). The emanation.

Shema, Shematteta ("Report"). Malkhut.

Shemesh ("Sun"). Tiferet.

Shanah ("Year"). Malkhut.

Shinui ("Change"). Malkhut in Metatron.

Shiur ("Measure"). The soul of the emanation.

Seorah ("Barley"). Malkhut.

Shualim ("Foxes"). *Kelipah.*

Sha'ar ("Gate"). Malkhut.

She'arim ("Gates"). The six "directions."

She'atnez ("Mixture" [linen and wool]). *Kelipah.*

Safah ("Tongue"). Malkhut.

Sak ("Sackcloth"). *Kelipah.*

Shekel ("Shekel"). Tiferet.

Sheker ("Falsehood"). Judgment.

Shekatot ("Troughs"). Neẓaḥ and Hod.

Sar ("Prince"). Malkhut, Metatron.

Sarah ("Princess," Sarah). Malkhut.

Sarim ("Princes"). Ḥokhmah, Binah.

Sharav ("Burning Heat"). Malkhut.

Serafim ("Seraphim"). Neẓaḥ and Hod.

Shesh Mashzar ("Fine Linen"). The totality [of sefirot].

Sasson ("Gladness"). Yesod.

Sheshet Yamim ("Six Days"). Tiferet.

Letter *Tav*

Ta'avah ("Desire"). Malkhut.

Te'omim ("Twins"). Neẓaḥ and Hod.

Tevu'ah ("Produce"). Malkhut.

Tevunah ("Understanding"), *Tohu* ("Formlessness"). Binah.

Tehillah ("Praise"). Keter, Ḥokhmah, Binah, Malkhut.

Tokh ("In the Midst"). Tiferet.

Tola'at ("Worm"), *Tosefta* ("Addition"), *Tor* ("Dove"). Malkhut.

Torah ("Torah"). Ḥokhmah, Binah, Tiferet, Malkhut.

Teḥum ("Boundary"), *Teḥinnah* ("Supplication"), *Teivah* ("Letter"). Malkhut.

Teyomet ("Central Leaf" [of palm branch]). Tiferet.

Teiku (undecided halakhah), *Tekhelet* ("Blue"). Malkhut.

Tel ("Mound"). Yesod.

Tam ("Innocent"), *Temunah* ("Image"). Malkhut.

Temurah ("Exchange"). In Yeẓirah.

Tamim ("Perfect"), *Temanta* ("Eight"). Malkhut.

Tamar ("Palm Tree"). Tiferet, Malkhut.

Tanaim (Mishnaic authorities). Neẓaḥ, Hod, Yesod.

Tinok ("Child"), *Tanin* ("Serpent"). Tiferet.

Teninim ha-Gedolim ("The Great Dragons" [Gen. 1:21]). The three "patriarchs." [56b]

Teudah ("Testimony"). Binah.

Tapuḥim ("Apples"). Neẓaḥ and Hod.

Tefillah ("Prayer"), *Tikvat Ḥut ha-Shani* ("Red Thread" [Josh. 2:18]). Malkhut.

Tekiah (Shofar blast). The Right [side of the sefirotic structure].

Teruah (Shofar blast). The Left [side of the sefirotic structure].

Takif ("Mighty"). Ḥesed.

Terumah ("Heave Offering"). Malkhut.

Tarshish (Tarshish). Ḥesed, Ḥasadim, Gevurah, Gevurot.

Teshuvah ("Repentance"). Binah.

May the glory of God endure forever. May the Lord rejoice in His works (Ps.104:31).

This work of heaven was completed on the fourth day [Wednesday], the *goodly gift* (Gen. 30:20) [= 13th] of Av the Merciful, [in the year] May [God] greatly restrain [*le-hashiv* = 347 (i.e., 5347, or 1587 in the civil calendar)] His anger and establish the Palace upon its rightful place.[24]

24. The "work of heaven" refers to the printing of the book, which was completed on Wednesday, 13 Av, 5347.

Appendix: The Introductory Material

1

TITLE PAGE

[1a]

The book
The Pleasant Light

[written] by the rabbi, the divine kabbalist, his honor, our teacher, rabbi Moses Cordovero, may his memory be a blessing.

[The book] is sweet for the soul and a healing for the bone, [a remedy] against the strange opinions described [therein] of those who distance themselves from the science of truth. *This is the gate of the Lord* (Ps. 118:20) in order that [we may] merit afterwards [the printing of] the book *'Or Yakar,*[1] which is the great light concerning the commentary of the Zohar.

The sixth section of this book is a glorious and praiseworthy abbreviation of the opinions which the rabbi, may his righteous memory be a blessing, dealt with at length in his youth in his book *Pardes Rimmonim.*[2]

1. Cordovero's commentary on the Zohar, *Or Yakar,* was not published until the twentieth century (Jerusalem, 1965 et seq.).

2. Cordovero completed *Pardes Rimmonim* at the age of twenty-seven.

2

INTRODUCTION BY MOSES BASSOLA

[1b]

Said the young man, Moses Bassola:[1]

It is incumbent upon me to praise the sage, his honor, our teacher, Rabbi Gedaliah,[2] son of the rabbi who authored [this work], may his righteous memory be a blessing. For he has kept the covenant of brotherhood and his old friendship [with me] in the Land of the Hart [Israel], may it be speedily rebuilt and established. He has brought me into the chamber of his learning and has stood me at his right hand to help and support him in order to raise the stumbling block from the path of this important book.

The *threefold thread* (Eccles. 4:12) with us is the great sage, the venerable and exalted Rabbi Israel, who works successfully with great might and power in the labor of printing honestly and for the sake of heaven. We have trusted, therefore, with God's mercy, that he will proofread properly, as he did in [the book] *Seder 'Avodat Yom ha-Kippurim*,[3] which was all his [work]. Mistakes are not found with him.

1. Bassola was a sixteenth-century Kabbalist, originally from Safed, who settled in Italy and collaborated with Gedaliah Cordovero on the publication of *Or Ne'erav* as well as Moses Cordovero's ethical treatise *Tomer Devorah* (Venice, 1589).

2. Gedaliah Cordovero (1562-1625), son of Moses Cordovero, was born in Safed. In Italy he collaborated with Moses Bassola and Menaḥem Azariah of Fano in the publication of various Kabbalistic treatises, including several by his father.

3. This was published in Venice in 1587.

To those who know may God be pleasant. May the blessing of heaven above come upon them.

[2a]

These are the words which Moses Bassola spoke when he saw [this] composition and its value and the *honor of* [its] *excellent majesty* (Esther 1:4):

All Israel has a place in the world of worthy souls which are cut out from under the throne[4] of Him who made the earth with His power and understanding, who *stretched forth the heavens* (Isa.44:24). *This is the blessing with which Moses, the man of God,*[5] *blessed the children of Israel* (Deut. 33:1) in order to purify their thoughts and to securely establish wisdom, and *to be enlightened with the light of the living* (Job 33:30). [However,] it was hidden from the eyes of the living until his son the sage,[6] may his Rock and Redeemer protect him, came and brought forth the sun from its place to bring light to the earth and those who dwell [there]. It is a treatise which princes have written. The benefactors of the people have said of it: Taste and see its sweetness and its worth. Every man should bear it in his desire and his bosom.

This is my portion from all my labor (Eccles. 2:10) to bring as a gift my poem of praise:

Go now, my songs, exultations, and poems
To praise and extol Him who formed abundances
And planted with wisdom His messengers in the Garden[7]

4. Cf. *Zohar Ḥadash* 24a.
5. A reference to Moses Cordovero.
6. A reference to Gedaliah Cordovero.
7. A reference to Cordovero's *Pardes Rimmonim.*

And caused this Light to shine to heal the flesh
Well and proper like the onyx and jasper.
It is Pleasant to all mouths like the honey of bees.
It was hidden away and concealed from the multitude
In the Land of the Hart, in inner chambers
Until Gedaliah came and said, "Let there be light,"
Like the clear sun causes light, and revealed the secrets. [2b]
Still I speak to my heart and continue to write:
Beloved, take *the Pleasant Light, as one who finds a great spoil* (Ps. 119:162).
[Written] by a great man, a rabbi like *a lion in the streets* (Prov. 26:13).
In it you will find secrets, it talks of exalted things
On the subject of [divine] attributes and the healing of thoughts.
[It speaks of] the secret of exalted Keter and Ḥokhmah, high in its hidden place,
Of Binah in the palanquin far and near.
Gedulah on the right, Gevurah bearing judgment
Like a mount of myrrh and frankincense and lofty walls.
The attribute of Tiferet is tied in the middle
And Neẓaḥ gathers the splinters in the path.
Hod and Yesod reveal to Malkhut, the bride,
And repeat and sit upon the pool.
In its midst is all wealth, in it is worthiness and uprightness
In the number ten [who are] *well favored and good* (Gen. 41:2).

[3a]

3

INTRODUCTION BY GEDALIAH CORDOVERO

Said the young man Gedaliah, son of my lord, my father, his honor, our teacher Rabbi Moses Cordovero, may his righteous memory be a blessing:

Since the time when God wondrously showed His lovingkindness to the holy man, my master and father, and came near to him in order to make the Torah great and to wondrously grant wisdom in the secret science [of Kabbalah], we have seen that his righteousness endures forever, encouraging the hearts of the students. Their eyes have been opened by his divine treatises. Their love [for them] continued until they merited to cease supporting the philosophical sciences, whose ways are darkness and sophistry. The righteous will be glad and rejoice in the science of the truth [so as to] walk before the Lord in the light of life.

This treatise is fine flour free of dirt which was sifted by the rabbi, my father and master, himself. He abbreviated the arguments which were expounded at length in the book *Pardes Rimmonim* which he wrote. He also included additional chapters at its beginning to cause to understand and to teach the usefulness of the science [of Kabbalah] and the necessity of studying it. I have seen that [this treatise] is found in many distinguished hands, even though I know that the rabbi did not edit it sufficiently, as he had intended to do. I was afraid that what happened to [his] commentary on the prayer of Rosh ha-Shanah would happen to it.[1] For it was stolen from me, and the one who printed it without my

1. It was published in Constantinople in 1576.

permission did not understand the intention of the author. Not only did he not correct what he found in his stolen [manuscript] from scribal errors, but he excised and diminished [the manuscript]. I hope, with God's mercy and aid, to be able to correct this iniquity.

Since [the opportunity] has come to our hands, I will say that after my teacher and father the rabbi, may his memory be a blessing, explained the reasons why we do not recite more than three "and therefores" in the blessings of the holiness of God during the Days of Awe,[2] according to the opinion of my mother's brother, the sage and pious rabbi Solomon ha-Levi Alkabetz,[3] he subsequently decided to say as well, "And therefore may it be sanctified," etc., according to the well-known version, for he found support [for this] in a section of the Zohar. This is also one of the omissions which should be inserted in the commentary.

When my soul yearned to [3b] begin editing this distinguished treatise, I found the worthy sage, Rabbi Menaḥem Azariah of Fano,[4] may the Merciful One guard and protect him, who was most faithful among all my father's household. He [my father] loved to write to him most of his teachings, and he [Menaḥem Azariah] adhered to them lovingly. He has already proceeded [in this work] and succeeded in editing [these teachings] and placing them in their proper place in entire agreement with what was clear to him concerning the intentions of the master in the rest of [his] compositions, which are more valuable than gold. In this manner he has also succeeded in an explication of the liturgy of Yom Kippur which the master had explained according to the method of the secret [doctrine].[5]

2. In the High Holiday liturgy, the three paragraphs after the Kedushah begin with the words "and therefore" (*uvekhen*).

3. Moses Cordovero's brother-in-law and teacher (ca. 1505-1584).

4. Italian rabbi and Kabbalist (1548-1620). He was the foremost exponent of Moses Cordovero's Kabbalistic system in Italy.

5. Published in Venice in 1587.

I saw [this] and directed my heart to [examine] all the detailed corrections, and they gave me joy. Concerning them I cited [the verse]: *He kisses the lips that give a right answer* (Prov. 24:26). *Therefore my heart is glad, and my glory rejoices* (Ps. 16:9). I have agreed to let the public benefit from them. *And though* our *beginning was small,* perhaps God will have mercy *and* our *end will greatly increase* (Job 8:7) for the sake of His glorious name. *May the graciousness of the Lord our God be upon us* (Ps. 90:17).

Amen, so may His will be.

4

EDITOR'S PREFACE

[4a]

Said the editor:[1]

This is God's camp (Gen. 32:3).[2] *The generation of those who seek Him* (Ps. 24:6) *will rejoice in His deeds* (Ps. 149:2) *like a dance of two companies* (Song of Songs 7:1). Our eyes have seen and were astonished [at these teachings] *arising out of the earth* (I Sam. 28:13) *to plant the heavens* (Isa. 51:16). Like the coming out of the sun at noontime, *a bright light is upon them* (Isa. 9:1). *The opening of* their *words gives light* (Ps. 119:130) and shines on a divine vision to those who are sanctified in the treasure-house of the secrets of Torah which is arrayed and guarded *from the lions' dens, from the mountains of leopards* (Song 4:8) [and] *overlaid with sapphires* (Song 5:14).

[My soul weeps] in secret places for your pride (Jer. 13:17) *and is faint all the day* (Lam. 1:13). The altar *of the wicked is an abomination* (Prov. 21:27). Yet despite this, *many waters cannot quench love* (Song 8:7), *for upright are the ways of the Lord* (Hos. 14:10). *He will judge the poor of the people* (Ps. 72:4), *He will establish peace* (Isa. 26:12). When He speaks *He will overcome the mighty* (Eccles. 10:10) for His people and His pious ones.

Does not wisdom cry out (Prov. 8:1) to the remnants of Israel *to observe discretion* (Prov. 2:11) [regarding] *the secrets of wisdom* (Job 11:6)? *They praise the Lord with their throats* (Ps. 149:6). In their

1. Presumably the Rabbi Israel referred to in Moses Bassola's introduction.

2. This preface, which is a pastiche of citations from the Bible and rabbinic literature, is exceedingly difficult to translate lucidly.

right hand is *fullness of joy* (Ps. 16:11) and pleasantness. They direct their tongue *with the pen of a ready writer* (Ps. 45:2) who has studied and understood. He is frightened by the fools among the people. They walk in darkness, refined in the smelter *of poverty and much servitude* (Lam. 1:3) *bordered with cords* (Esther 1:6) of mockery, folly, and ignorance in *the captivity of this host* (Obad. 1:20) *when vileness is exalted among the sons of men* (Ps. 12:9). They are ignorant of the time to plant *the tree of life in the midst of the garden* (Gen. 2:9)

For from the quarrelsome words of the immature grain, a thorn has spread among the brethren *and rebellion like the sin of witchcraft* (I Sam. 15:23). *When the time comes she raises her wings on high* (Job 39:18). *God know the days of the perfect* (Ps. 37:18) *and the way of the righteous* (Ps. 1:6), and *raises up from the dust* (Ps. 113:7) and *the far distant sea* (Ps. 65:6) *all the souls of the house of Jacob* (Gen. 46:27). They all eagerly desire to hear the word of God *and the ancient records* (I Chron. 4:22). However, [until] now they have not seen the clear light of [Him who dwells] in the skies. *For from the top of the Rocks I see Him* (Num. 23:9), *and among those who turn the many to righteousness* (Dan. 12:3) *I behold Him. Grace is poured upon* their *lips* (Ps. 45:3) [4b] *like roses* (Song 5:13). Their waters are more sure than *the garden spring, a well of living waters* (Song 4:15). *Like doves [going] to their cotes* (Isa. 60:8) they have drunk spices. *They call to God, and He answers them* (Ps. 99:6). *This one says, I am the Lord's* (Isa. 44:5), *answer me with broad spaces* (Ps. 118:5), for my *heart does not rest at night* (Eccles. 2;23), *nor does my spirit within me* (Isa. 26:9). *This one writes with his hand to the Lord* (Isa. 44:5) from that which had preceded him [at] Sinai, and on the *skins of kid goats* (Gen. 27:16) *they set up their signs* (Ps. 74:4) which they wrote to instruct them *for their generations, an eternal covenant* (Exod. 31:16).

From afar the Most High (Ps. 138:6) has established a decree and has bequeathed of His wisdom to those who fear Him. *His lightnings, judgments, and laws* will *light up* (Ps. 97:4) *to open blinded eyes* (Isa. 42:7) which have never seen the light of Your heavens. They fall and err in mockery. *Far from men they swing* (Job 28:4), as in a desert.

Let the deaf hear (Isa. 42:18) and the lame run and not get tired. *Let the blind see* (Isa. 42:18) the *teeming visions* (Exod. 38:8) which are gleaned and reaped by *the heads of the tribes* (Num. 30:2), *they and their children* (Gen. 33:6), commoner and priest alike, as is acknowledged properly. "All is foreseen, and permission is given" (Avot 3:16). *Let the men go* (Exod. 10:11) *to the chief cornerstone* (Ps. 118:22) *to make books* (Eccles. 12:12) which speak of the honor of God to the house of Israel. *For all the congregation* (Num. 16:3), *the suckling with the venerable man* (Deut. 32:25), *and the mixed multitude fell a lusting* (Num. 11:4) *for Torah and testimony* (Isa. 8:20), *and the weaned child shall put his hand* (Isa. 11:8).

And I heard behind me (Ezek. 3:12) a herald calling. Will you not answer [that] I will prepare my generation, for you have not denied the words of the Master of the Earth, [who is] awesome in praise in the darkness, *and light dwells with Him* (Dan. 2:22). *I will tell of the decree* (Ps. 2:7), advice from afar. Indeed, these are the lambs of the Merciful One, *the eternal God [who] is a dwelling-place* (Deut. 33:27), Selah. *Why should you ask, when it is miraculous?* (Judg. 13:18). *The Lord of Hosts has purposed, and who will disannul it?* (Isa. 14:27). *If I would relate and speak of them, they are more than can be told* (Ps. 40:6), *for it is to test* (Exod. 20:20) us *that He orders His angels* (Ps. 91:11) for us *in the high heavens above and on the earth below* (Deut. 4:39). *They sanctify and purify themselves* (Isa. 66:17) to comprehend the rash and to give merit to the multitude concerning the things that are the mysteries of the world, *to bring all hidden things to judgment* (Eccles. 12:14), for thus it arose in [His] thought, and it is known to all that *there is a time and a season for each thing* (Eccles. 3:1), *and snarl against all sound wisdom* (Prov. 18:1), and [for] the enlightened one [who wishes] to do well, his silence suffices for him. Let him be [more] silent for the Lord than the roar of the [5a] lion [is loud]. He will place and desire, and his heart will understand that not all faces are alike, *and [that] God has made high and uplifted* (Isa. 57:15) lowly and dark, both essential and nonessential, [so] *that they should fear Him* (Eccles. 3:14). For the *mem* and the *samekh* on the [stone] tablets are still suspended and stand. They warn and testify as a sign and anger [that will] consume and destroy those who utilize the crown not for its own sake,[3] with a deadly poison for those who defy her will. *A contemptible brand in the thought of him that is at ease* (Job 12:5) *under every leafy tree* (Deut. 12:2).

It is the medicine of life for those who find it on *all that comes out of the mouth of God* (Deut. 8:3), who *has given a banner to those who fear You that it may be displayed because of the truth, Selah* (Ps. 60:6).

How much more so will *he who fears the Lord* (Exod. 9:20) give more love, awe, fear, and humility, will he worry because of his sins, and will he be concerned lest he increase his sins with the iniquity of erring in the statements [concerning] the knowledge of the *holy God* (Josh. 24:19) lest *his soul offer itself in restitution* (Isa. 53:10). *His only recourse* (Esther 4:11) and *the territory of his inheritance* (Deut. 32:9) is to strip himself, and to cut and offer [himself] as a complete sin offering. He will be morally strong *to bind with a bond forbidding* (Num. 30:3) that which he has not

3. Cf. Mishnah, Avot 1:13.

heard from his teachers. *He makes even all his paths* (Prov. 5:21) *and the utterances of his lips* (Ps. 21:3). For *if he falls* (Deut. 22:8), *who will raise him up?* (Gen. 49:9). *The Lord alone will lead him, and there is no strange god with him* (Deut. 31:12) who has apportioned to test in them *and afflicted* [them] *because of their iniquities* (Ps. 107:17).

How has become dim (Lam. 4:1) for them *the candle of commandment and the light of Torah* (Prov. 6:23) which gives light to these hypocrites. *For like the grass they will soon wither* (Ps. 37:2), since a mistake in learning causes intentional sin, *Sheol and Abaddon* (Prov. 15:11), *the venom of serpents and the poison of vipers* (Deut. 32:33). *But they are altogether brutish and foolish* (Jer. 10:8), [following] *after vanity, and they will become naught* (Jer. 2:5), attempting to bring forth a *perverted justice* (Hab. 1:4) which will eventuate in a defective deed. *Turn away from the tents* (Num. 16:26) of the man who slumbers, the *ass of a wild man* (Job 11:12); a fool and ignorant man is his companion, *brutish, unlike a man* (Prov. 30:2), who errs and is like a fool.

Have I not said to you, *I shall be clear* (Ps. 19:14), for he will *be a healer* (Isa. 3:7)? He who utilizes the Daughter of a Voice will become rich. There is none *who aggrandizes himself to say* (I Kings 1:5), learn Gemara. And *if he is a poor man, he sleeps on his pledge* (Deut. 24:12) *and rides on a donkey* (Zech. 9:9); he glorifies himself in the hidden wisdom *and its tumult, and delights in it* (Isa. 5:14). *There is no spirit within him* (Hab. 2:19), *and the living will take it to heart* (Eccles. 7:2), *for with stratagems will we wage war* (Prov. 24:6), [5b] with *a fortiori* [reasoning] and equivalent statements in the bundles of Mishnah, *and from the desert a gift* (Num. 21:18) [by] *which man will live* (Ps. 89:49), *if he will be as a horse or a donkey not to understand* (Ps. 32:9) the laws of God, positive and negative. *He tells his words; in keeping them there is great reward* (Ps. 19:12) to complete their commandments in the most acceptable way.

Tomorrow God will perform *righteous acts for His nobles* (Judg. 5:11). *Those who serve Him, who do His will* (Ps. 103:21), *over all the glory is a canopy* (Isa. 4:5). He will spread a cloth for the feast of the Leviathan *in the courtyard of the garden of the palace* (Esther 1:5). All will bend from reciting and bowing *a psalm of thanksgiving* (Ps. 100:1), for the merit of his fellow when *he shined his lamp* (Job 29:3) his inside is like his outside as he is there. *Eternal joy is upon their heads* (Isa. 35:10), *each sharpening the countenance of his fellow* (Prov. 27:17). All this has God wrought for His own sake. *He will rescue him and honor him* (Ps. 91:15). *He will spread the cloud of His lightning* (Job 37:11) upon the head of the Eternal Righteous One, *and upon him he will place His crown* (Ps. 132:18).

This is the advice necessary for *the man whom the king wishes to honor* (Esther 6:6). Peace of mind to *the poor and lowly of spirit, who trembles at His word* (Isa. 66:2). *Let him not boast of the morrow* (Prov. 27:1), "for the reward of [the performance of] a commandment is a commandment" (Avot 4:2). *He desired it for his habitation* (Ps. 132:13); *until the day breathe* (Song 2:17) *man will go out to his labor* (Ps. 104:23), [which] *will be accepted for him* (Lev. 1:4), *his fruit in its time* (Ps. 1:3). *This tarrying in the house for a little* (Ruth 2:7), *for the command of the king was urgent* (I Sam. 21:9). Prepare outside *your sword and your bow* (Gen. 27:3), *and do all your labor* (Exod. 20:9) in Scripture, Mishnah, and Gemara, and there will be stored for you in the field of apples[4] a heap of good deeds. Afterwards you will build your house "as a meeting house for the sages" (Avot 1:4), *numerous and perfect* (Nah. 1:12),

4. The "apple trees" symbolize the sefirot from Gedulah to Yesod. Malkhut is called the "Field of Apples" because she is filled with "apple trees."

seated upon judgment seats (Judg. 5:10) in holiness, and receiving one from another in whispers, crowned with their tefillin and *fringes which they make for themselves* (Deut. 22:12) to wrap themselves with awe and fear. They seclude themselves like *standing Seraphim* (Isa. 6:2), *like brethren sitting together* (Ps. 133:1). And if, *as God lives* (I Sam. 20:3), they speak of *the face of the eagle* (Ezek. 1:10), *they were swifter and stronger than lions* (I Samuel 1:23), *and the noise of the wings of the living creatures* (Ezek. 3:13) says, *Blessed be the glory of God* (Ezek. 3:12), *who loves righteousness* (Ps. 11:7), and the words rejoice as when they were given at Sinai *from before God, the Lord of all the earth* (Josh. 3:13).

Hear me, my brothers, and give ear to me, my people (I Chron. 28:2). *Understand, you fools* (Prov. 8:5); listen, you rulers. Be careful what you say, *and may God be with you* (Gen. 48:21). If [6a] [you see] scholars in a vision like rams butting and vanquishing each other,[5] it is not for you or us to say, "*Remember and observe*:[6] this tradition is proper, and that tradition is improper." *Solutions are for God* (Gen. 40:8). Those who are basing [their belief] upon *the explanation of a thing* (Eccles. 8:1), *not to fan and not to cleanse* (Jer. 4:11). *Is there not a time of service for man upon the earth?* (Job 7:1), *while the testimony of God is faithful* (Ps. 19:8), as is known to an ear which hears. *You who dwell in the gardens, friends listen* (Song 8:13), *you will lie down in the midst of the wise* (Prov. 15:31).

If the spirit which rules all fails and they prophesy, my words will be fulfilled *on those who rise against me* (Ps. 92:12). *Is Saul also among the prophets?* (I Sam. 10:11). This you will answer, *And who is their father?* (I Sam. 10:12). These things go after the

5. Cf. Dan. 8.

6. Cf. Rashi on Exod. 20:8, regarding the difference in the text of the Ten Commandments in Exodus and Deuteronomy.

intention of the heart. *I, in my innocence* (Ps. 26:1), plead before my judges: Let him judge all the words of this epistle leniently in its quantity and quality. *If my soul does not speak from worry* (Josh. 22:24), consider me as one who mentions and reminds the enlightened ones of *my bountiful nation* (Song 6:12). "Dear is man, who was created in [God's] image" (Avot 3:15). *Speaking as a righteous company* (Ps. 58:2), He will judge righteousness. *For my heart is not haughty* (Ps. 131:1), all *my senses are in me* (Job 20:2), *and my eyes are not haughty* (Ps. 131:1) *before the God of Sinai* (Ps, 68:9). *I have not walked in greatness or wonders* (Ps. 131:1) *with the King, the Lord of Hosts* (Isa. 6:5). For the maidservant has seen[7] and *is more righteous than I* (Gen. 38:26). *I am lighter* [in consequence] *than she is* (II Sam. 6:22). I *am lower than the earth* (Isa. 29:4). I speak in honor of our God, *who dwells in Zion* (Josh. 4:21). *And He, being merciful, will forgive* [my] *sin* (Ps. 78:38).

7. The reference is to the midrash which states that a maidservant at the parting of the Red Sea saw more than the prophet Ezekiel in his visions. Cf. Mekhilta, Shirta 3.

BIBLIOGRAPHY

General Works on Kabbalah

Blau, Joseph L. *The Christian Interpretation of the Cabala in the Renaissance.* New York, 1944.

Cohen, M. S. *The Shiur Qomah.* Lanham, Md., 1983.

Dan, Joseph. *Ha-Mistikah ha-'Ivrit ha-Kedumah.* Tel-Aviv, 1989.

———. *Jewish Mysticism and Jewish Ethics.* Seattle, 1986.

———. "Midrash and the Dawn of Kabbalah." In *Midrash and Literature,* edited by G. Hartman and S. Budick, pp. 127-139. New Haven, 1986.

Gruenwald, Itamar. "From Talmudic to Zoharic Hermeneutics" [Hebrew]. *Jerusalem Studies in Jewish Thought* 8 (1989): 255-298.

Idel, Moshe. *Kabbalah: New Perspectives.* New Haven, 1988.

———. "On the History of the Interdiction Against the Study of Kabbalah Before the Age of Forty" [Hebrew]. *AJS Review* 5 (1980): 1-20 (Hebrew pagination).

———. "We Have No Tradition on This." In *Nahmanides*, edited by Isadore Twersky. Cambridge, Mass., 1983.

Kaplan, Aryeh. *Sefer Yezirah: The Book of Creation.* York Beach, Maine, 1990.

Liebes, Yehuda. "Ha-Mashiaḥ shel ha-Zohar." In *The Messianic Idea in Jewish Thought*, pp. 87-236. Jerusalem, 1977.

———. "How the Zohar Was Written" [Hebrew]. *Jerusalem Studies in Jewish Thought* 8 (1989): 1-72.

———. *Perakim be-Millon Sefer ha-Zohar.* Jerusalem, 1982.

Matt, Daniel, "The Mystic and the Mizvot." In *Jewish Spirituality from the Bible to the Middle Ages*, ed. Arthur Green. New York, 1987.

———. *Zohar: The Book of Enlightenment.* New York, 1983.

Scholem, Gershom. *Jewish Gnosticism, Merkabah Mysticism and the Talmudic Tradition.* New York, 1965.

———. *Kabbalah.* New York, 1974.

———. *Major Trends in Jewish Mysticism.* New York, 1941.

———. *On the Kabbalah and Its Symbolism.* New York, 1969.

———. *Origins of the Kabbalah.* Philadelphia, 1987.

Tishby, Isaiah. *Mishnat ha-Zohar.* 2 vols. Jerusalem, 1957.

Verman, Mark. "The Development of *Yihudim* in Spanish Kabbalah." *Jerusalem Studies in Jewish Thought* 8 (1989): 25-42 (English sec.).

———."Mysticism, Indoctrination and Society." Paper presented at conference at University of British Columbia, 1988.

Wolfson, Elliot. "By Way of Truth: Aspects of Naḥmanides' Kabbalistic Hermeneutic." *AJS Review* 14 (1989): 103-178.

———. "Circumcision and the Divine Name." *Jewish Quarterly Review* 78 (1987): 77-112.

———. "Circumcision, Vision of God, and Textual Interpretation: From Midrashic Trope to Mystical Symbol." *History of Religions* 27 (1987): 189-215.

———. "Letter Symbolism and Anthropomorphic Imagery in the Zohar." *Jerusalem Studies in Jewish Thought* 8 (1989).

———. "Mystical Rationalization of the Commandments in *Sefer ha-Rimmon.*" *Hebrew Union College Annual* 59 (1988): 217-251.

The Sixteenth Century

Fine, Lawrence. *Safed Spirituality: Rules of Mystical Piety and the Beginning of Wisdom.* New York, 1984.

Goetschel, Roland. *Meir Ibn Gabbay, Le Discours de la Kabbale Espagnole.* Louvain, 1981.

Gries, Zev. "Iẓẓuv Safrut ha-Hanhagot ha-Ivrit be-Mifneh ha-Me'ah ha-Shesh Esreh uva-Me'ah ha-Shva Esreh u-Mashmauto ha-Historit." *Tarbiz* 56 (1987): 527-581.

Horowitz, Elliot. "Coffee, Coffeehouses and the Nocturnal Rituals of Early Modern Jewry." *AJS Review* 14 (1989): 17-46.

Idel, Moshe. "One from a Town, Two from a Clan: The Question of the Diffusion of Lurianic Kabbalah and Sabbatianism; A Reexamination." Paper presented at conference at Harvard University, 1988.

Katz, Jacob. "Maḥloket ha-Semikhah beyn Rabbi Yaakov Berab veha-Ralbaḥ." *Zion* 16 (1951): 28-45.

Meroz, Ronit. "Redemption in the Lurianic Teaching" [Hebrew]. Ph.D. diss., Hebrew University, 1988.

Pachter, Mordecai. "Elijah de Vidas' *Beginning of Wisdom* and Its Abbreviated Versions" [Hebrew]. *Kiryat Sefer* 47 (1972): 686-710.

Robinson, Ira. "Abraham ben Eliezer Halevi: Kabbalist and Messianic Visionary of the Early Sixteenth Century." Ph.D. diss., Harvard University, 1980.

———. "Halakha, Kabbala and Philosophy in the Thought of Joseph Jabez." *Studies in Religion* 11 (1982): 389-402.

Ruderman, David. *Kabbalah, Magic and Science: the Cultural Universe of a Sixteenth Century Jewish Physician.* Cambridge, Mass., 1988.

Schechter, Solomon. "Safed in the Sixteenth Century." In *Studies in Judaism,* Second Series. Philadelphia, 1908.

Tishby, Isaiah. "Ha-Pulmus 'al Sefer ha-Zohar be-Me'ah ha-Shesh-Esreh be-Italiyah." In *Studies of Kabbalah and Its Branches,* vol. 1. Jerusalem, 1982.

Werblowsky, R. J. Z. *Joseph Karo: Lawyer and Mystic.* Oxford, 1962.

Zak, Beracha. "Torat ha-Sod shel R. Shelomo Alkabetz." Ph.D. diss., Brandeis University, 1977.

Other Works by Moses Cordovero

Elimah Rabbati. Brody, 1881.

Gerushin. Venice, ca. 1602.

Or Yakar. Jerusalem, 1965 et seq.

Pardes Rimmonim. 1st edition, 1592; edition consulted, Jerusalem, 1962.

Perush le-Tefillat Rosh ha-Shanah. Constantinople, 1576.

Seder 'Avodat Yom ha-Kippurim. Venice, 1587.

Shiur Komah. 1883.

Tomer Devorah. Venice, 1589.

Jacobs, Louis, ed. and trans. *The Palm Tree of Deborah.* New York, 1981.

Editions of *Or Ne'erav*

Venice, 1587.

Cracow, 1647.

Fuerth, 1701.

Zolkiev, 1780.

Zolkiev, 1851.

Vilna, 1885.

Tel-Aviv, 1965.

Jerusalem, 1989.

Commentaries and Studies on Cordovero

Ben-Shlomo, Yosef. *The Mystical Theology of Moses Cordovero* [Hebrew]. Jerusalem, 1986.

Gallico, Samuel. *Assis Rimmonim.* Venice, 1601.

Menaḥem Azariah of Fano. *Pelaḥ ha-Rimmon.* Venice, 1600.

Robinson, Ira. "Moses Cordovero and Kabbalistic Education in the Sixteenth Century." *Judaism* 39 (1990): 155-162.

Zak, Bracha. "Galut Yisrael ve-Galut ha-Shekhinah be-*Or Yakar* le-Rabbi Mosheh Cordovero." *Meḥkarei Yerushalayim be-Maḥshevet Yisrael* 1 (1982).

———. "Shelosha Zemanei Geulah be-*Or Yakar* le-Rabbi Mosheh Cordovero." In *Meshiḥiyut va-Eschatologiah*, ed. Z. Bares, pp. 281-293. Jerusalem, 1984.

Index